Tokyo

FOR

Food

Lovers

JONAS CRAMBY

Hardie Grant

TRAVEL

CONTENTS

Introduction 5
  Disclaimer
  Some advice for you,
    the reader
Ramen & tsukemen 10
Udon, soba & tempura 24
Yakiniku 36
Yakitori & yakiton 50
Japanese curry 62
Gyoza & biru 72
Tonkatsu 82

Sushi 93
Izakaya 100
Fast food & sweet
  treats 112
Coffee & tea 128
Craft beer, natural wine
  & sake 150
Japanese bars 162
Practicalities 172
Index 174

DISCLAIMER

It is actually impossible to write a restaurant guide for Tokyo. First of all, there are over 150,000 restaurants in the city – compare that with New York, which is said to have about 10,000 food outlets. When you then consider that a large percentage of these 150,000 restaurants are actually good – no, fantastic – than in any other city in the world, you soon realize that Tokyo's food culture is so multidimensional that you could be mistaken for thinking there is more than one city, depending on what kind of food lover you talk to.

Let me explain. There is a Tokyo for those who like Michelin-starred restaurants, another for those interested in craft beer and yet another if you like sushi. If you are in to Django Reinhardt, you will experience completely different things than if you are interested in manga and cosplay. Therefore, it is useless to even try to answer the question I've been asked at least once a week over the past three years: "Okay, which are, hands down, the three best restaurants in Tokyo?"

Had that question been about Stockholm, I could probably have answered it. Yes, maybe even London or New York. But asking this question about Tokyo is like asking which three websites are the best on the internet.

It is simply impossible to answer. So, to get the most out of this book, it is important that you understand that it is not the final guide to this culinary megacity, but more a reflection of the best of my personal interests, obsessions and hang-ups. First of all, I am a person who hates to make a fool of myself. I am a nervous and paranoid traveler who detests not knowing how you're expected to behave in every single situation. Therefore, I have tried to include so many instructions for like-minded travelers that an alternative title to this book could have been *A social phobic's guide to the world's most difficult-to-understand foodie city*.

It wasn't that long ago, I traveled to Tokyo for the first time, but I have since then been there many times. I don't have a deep knowledge of Japan but I have a good intuition – which I am not afraid to use – and my girlfriend is an academically trained East Asia expert – so really, her knowledge and assistance has meant that she really should have been a co-author of this book (an offer that she declined).

In terms of food, I am actually more fascinated by emerging or established food scenes, such as the hipster generation's embrace of folksy Japanese curry, than getting a table at the city's most sought after restaurants. I always plan my trips around what I want to eat and get pissed off if I am forced to have lunch at some shit place for practical reasons. I'd rather queue than book a table, and I don't mind traveling long distances for a bowl of ramen.

I probably suffer from an unhealthy fondness for alcohol. I'm not bothered by hipsters, I love their sense of quality, and really hope I don't see food as a status symbol – but I'm pretty blind to price tags and can burn money like a comet rushing towards Earth. I am aware of the problems that come with "exotification", while I myself cannot help but romanticize Japan mainly for three reasons: I saw the movie *Blade Runner* as a child, listened to Japanese punk rock as a teenager and as an adult I meditate and study Zen Buddhism.

I love narrow alleys, smoky yakiniku places, steamy ramen pubs, wardrobe-size cocktail bars and eating lunch in the local convenience store. I like main dishes better than desserts, grilled more than steamed, crispy more than soft, cold more than lukewarm and I get a warm fuzzy feeling from neon signs that are reflected in rain-wet asphalt.

I hope that these basic facts about me can help you use the tips in this book as a set of keys no, lock picks, to your own, personal Tokyo. This is how you do it:

1. Read the book carefully and then go to a place that interests you.
2. Once there, try to find other similar places by looking for flyers or talking to staff and other guests.
3. Go to the new place, repeat step two and then continue as you go deeper and deeper into the matrix until you have created your own alternative Tokyo reality.

SOME ADVICE FOR YOU, THE READER

The reason you are browsing this book right now, I guess, is that you are eager to travel to Tokyo. You're not alone. Japan is one of the world's fastest growing travel destinations with an annual increase of about 33 percent. They are expected to double their tourism from around 20 million visitors in 2015 to nearly 40 million during the Olympic Games in 2020. This is of course good news for tourist councils and municipal politicians.

Less so for us foodies.

There are already restaurants in Tokyo that choose not to serve tourists.

The reason for this is not some kind of vague xenophobia, but instead because the restaurant culture in Japan simply doesn't always work like it does in the west. There are misunderstandings and pub-culture clashes and so it may be easier for the owners to claim that the place is fully booked. It is not about any advanced etiquette rules, just that you shouldn't behave like an asshole. Because if all of us new visitors to Japan don't develop a certain cultural sensitivity, in the worst case, Tokyo's pub life risks being divided into two: one for tourists and one for locals.

And I would hate if this book should contribute to that development.

Therefore, I thought I'd offer you some strong advice.

1. If you book a table, show up

In Buddhism, there is a bodhisattva promise that says that you should "save all living beings". In Japan, they seem to have added "... from themselves". This means that you don't gain benefits for yourself at the expense of others. You have respect for others' personal space, time and integrity. This permeates the whole culture and makes it unthinkable that someone should jump queues, take anything that is not offered or simply not show up for a table booking. So if you have booked a table, make sure you show up. It is so simple. It doesn't matter that you may have found a better place or that you will never meet the owners again. The point is that if you don't show up for your booking the next time a tourist tries to book the same restaurant they might get a "no". So you have something of a responsibility for all of us visitors to Japan. In Japanese foodie culture it is also expected that you arrive on time, even preferably five minutes before a booking.

2. Eat what is offered

In the west, people aren't defined by what they eat but rather by what they DON'T eat. Wherever people go they expect that there should always be a vegetarian/gluten-free/organic alternative. It doesn't really work that way in Japan. It is not that you can't get these things, just that it is you who does the work by choosing where to go. If you are a vegetarian, for example, maybe you shouldn't go to a yakiniku place; if you don't eat raw fish you should probably avoid sushi; and if you go to a pub that serves *horumon* (pork offal), you'll have to happily eat that fried pork rectum*.

* Maybe you don't have to do just that, but you know what I mean.

3. Don't be so easily offended

I usually say that Tokyo is a city with inverted Yelp ratings, so if a place has a lot of zero-star reviews and indignant comments from various tourists, then it's probably great. Because many tourists get extremely offended when they encounter a restaurant owner with integrity. We are indoctrinated to believe that service is everything and that the customer is always right. But they aren't. Fact is that at some of the best places it's the other way around. Because Japan's long history of Zen Buddhism has given rise to a culture of *shokunins* (artisans) who all dedicate themselves wholeheartedly and diligently to the narrow life that lies before them.

For these artisans, their daily work is a kind of mindfulness in action, and this doesn't just apply to celebrated sushi and *kaiseki* chefs but also to the person who pours your coffee, mixes your drink, grills your yakiniku skewer or wraps up your newly purchased chef's knife. The fact that they have dedicated their lives to their craft actually means that *they* know best. Not you. And if you can't appreciate that, maybe you should travel somewhere else.

4. Don't be so extroverted

When planning a trip to Tokyo, the most important thing is not when or how you get there. But instead how many people are in your group. I can't think of a less suitable city for a rowdy bunch of drunken louts to vacation in. In Tokyo the ideal is to travel in small groups of two people. Partly because of purely physical limitations, like how most pubs have around a total of six seats, and partly because it is a city to approach conscientiously.

Instead of barging into a place as if you own the world, politely stick your head inside, hold up as many fingers as you are people in your group and if you are invited in, get a sense of the place before you start taking pictures, talking on the phone, laughing loudly and messing around. Maybe it's a place where this is welcomed, maybe it's not. Quite simply, show some sensitivity to others.

In Tokyo, it is actually an advantage to be a little introverted, shy and self-conscious. It is GOOD to be a person who hates to make a fool of themselves. It's a city where it's the extroverted, loud, aggressive people that are odd. Maybe that's why I love it so much. Or maybe it's the tonkatsu. I don't know.

RAMEN & TSUKEMEN

The world's best noodle soup

There are roughly 50,000 ramen places in Japan, which I assume makes them the East Asian equivalent to McDonald's. That is if your local McDonald's had a two-hour long line and the hamburger was placed in the bread by a mindfulness coach.

Because in Japan, ramen is more a national obsession than a fast food: there are ramen bloggers, ramen movies, ramen fanatics, ramen manga, even a ramen museum. And it is standard procedure to line up for 30 minutes at your favorite

place, and up to three or four hours if it is an especially popular restaurant, such as the two ramen restaurants in Tokyo that were awarded Michelin stars. And all this is for a dish that costs around US$8 and takes about 5 minutes to eat.

As someone who mostly eats instant ramen and is generally suspicious of soup – which everyone knows is the most boring food – I understand that this might sound strange, but saying ramen is a soup is a bit like calling a wedding cake a cupcake. It is so much more! As for ramen being a traditional "fast food", because it is fast to make, it definitely is not a dish to be sneered at. For an average ramen chef making ramen is his entire life. Making ramen is an art, and unlike many other things in tradition-driven Japanese culture, there is room for innovation and personality. Then of course, ramen is good too. Ridiculously good. Bending over a steaming bowl of ramen with a smile on your lips, a little oil around your mouth and noodles hanging like a delicate kind of goatee from your chin is a blissful and, in fact, a mandatory Tokyo experience.

It's an experience that happens to suit the first-time visitor well because in Tokyo it's easy to feel a little lost. English-speaking waiters and English menus are not as

common as in other countries, and Japanese etiquette can sometimes seem confusing. But ordering a bowl of ramen is something most visitors can handle. You don't even have to talk to anyone, just press a button, hand over your tickets and smile politely.

Outside the ramen restaurants, there are usually machines where you order and pay for food, drinks and extra toppings. On most machines there are pictures of the food, but if the machine just has Japanese writing on it, just live a little dangerously and order the same as the person in front of you. When you've paid you take the tickets and sit down where there's space. A staff member will come to take your ticket. Hand it to them with both hands – it's polite.

When the ice-cold beer that you ordered is served, take a sip, lean back and observe the beautiful ramen ballet taking place in the kitchen in front of you.

When your soup arrives, all that's left is to dig in, and quickly – one bowl should preferably be eaten in 6–10 minutes; partly to make room for the others in the line, partly so the noodles don't get overcooked in the hot broth. A ramen shop is not a place where you hang out for hours with a beer, but a quick pit stop where you are in and out in minutes. Lean over the soup, lift some noodles with the chopsticks and slurp them into your mouth as loudly as you can. This way it tastes better and the noodles are cooled down. Yes, it is almost impolite to eat too quietly. Follow the noodle slurping by drinking the broth with the spoon and picking up the toppings and taking a bite – it's okay to put things back in the soup, but don't stir it. And the egg is always eaten with the spoon. When you are finished, you bow, say "*Gochisousama*" (It was delicious) and walk away with a litre of happiness sloshing around in your stomach.

Nakiryu

If you like fine dining on a budget, you need to go to Otsuka in northern Tokyo. This is the location of the two ramen places with Michelin stars: **Tsuta** and Nakiryu. If you plan to visit, you will need to arrive at least a few hours early, partly because the area is quite far from everything else, partly because of the queues. About an hour before opening, Nakiryu is already full of diners, and a special "queue" manager keeps track of all the ramen-hungry people. There are four separate queues and you move forward only when you are told to. Only real newbies change queues themselves or go straight ahead and yank the door open – queue jumping is an unknown concept in this part of the world. But because the line is so organized and people eat their ramen so fast, it also becomes quite ok to wait: no offended sighs, no one pushing in, no risk of not getting any noodles; just tummies rumbling in anticipation of yummy ramen. Is it worth it? Yes!

As soon as you enter Nakiryu, your boredom vanishes and you experience an attentive service that is much like traditional fine dining. Even the food has that flair that reveals a *shokunin* (an artisan) is at work. Despite the Michelin star, Nakiryu is priced like a regular ramen shop, at about US$8 per portion. They have the usual *shoyu* and *shio* ramen, (p. 20), although the specialty is their fantastic *dandan* noodles – look for 担々麺 on the ramen machine. Inspired by the Sichuan noodles of the same name, they consist of perfectly cooked, handmade wheat noodles with pork mince in a hot, beautiful, bright-orange broth.

~~~~~~ FACTS ~~~~~~

THE SYSTEM OF THE JAPANESE RAMEN QUEUE

* (see picture above)

1 A security guard ensures the people in the queue don't disrupt traffic.

2 The restaurant's "queue manager" on his way to take people from queue 1 (not in picture) to queue 2 (see point 3).

3 Queue 2.

4 Queue 3, mistaken by many newbies to be queue 1.

5 Queue 4, the so-called "bench queue".

Afuri

Afuri is so popular that there are now nine Afuri siblings in Tokyo (and one in Portland, USA). But the original is in Ebisu, and a visit here is mandatory for serious ramen lovers. Afuri makes a modern kind of ramen that may not necessarily be good for you, but definitely tastes like it is. It is clean, simple and their specialty flavored with yuzu (a Japanese citrus fruit) is fresh like a spring creek.

The water used in the broth is even said to come from a spring on the mountain Afuri in Kanagawa, hence the name. They have an English menu and it is generally easy for first-time visitors to order.

o Open every day 11am–5pm

d Ebisu

a F 117 Building, 1-1-7 Ebisu

Kikanbo

When traveling back to a favorite city, the same dilemma always arises for us foodies: should we try new places or go back to old favorites? This choice is made more difficult in Tokyo, because there are so many restaurants, many of which are really good. One place I always return to is Kikanbo. They may not have Tokyo's best ramen, but it is the kind I constantly have a low-intensity craving for, which only gets stronger the closer I get to Akihabara.

In addition to the usual pork, eggs and noodles, it consists of an extremely rich pork and miso broth which is seasoned Sichuan-style with two types of heat: *kara* (chili) and *shibi* (sansho pepper). This is then topped with a high pile of flash-fried bean sprouts. Next door to the ramen shop is Kikanbo's tsukemen restaurant which is just as good, making it hard to choose between them.

- Open Monday to Saturday 11am–9.30pm, Sunday 11am–4pm
- Akihabara
- 2-10-9 Kajicho

Rokurinsha

Inside Tokyo Station is Tokyo Ramen Street – a long indoor street filled with lots of restaurants. The most legendary, and allegedly chef David Chang's favorite venue, is Rokurinsha. Here they serve the ramen variant tsukemen – thicker, chewier noodles, served in a separate bowl to the broth, which itself is thicker and tastier than the usual broth. You dip some noodles into the broth and then eat them. Lovely! Rokurinsha also has a branch at Haneda airport, which means that Haneda has replaced Narita as my airport of choice in Tokyo.

- 🕐 Open every day 7.30–9.45am and 10.30am–10.45pm
- 📍 Chiyoda
- 📌 Tokyo Ramen Street, Tokyo Station

----- FACTS -----

TOKYO RAMEN STREET

Tokyo Ramen Street consists of eight ramen shops and is a part of Kitchen Street – a huge dining area in Tokyo Station. Here you could spend the rest of your life without getting bored of all the food that's on offer. It is also a practical alternative for the traveler, since you often pass Tokyo Station on your way to other places anyway. You find Kitchen Street by going to the first floor of Tokyo Station and then heading towards Yaesu North exit.

Konjiki Hototogisu

Hototogisu is the Japanese name for the lesser cuckoo, and that is precisely how you can feel when you eat here – a little cuckoo. Konjiki Hototogisu has neither an English-language ramen machine nor English-speaking staff, and is so remote that the customers mostly consist of slurping locals. And it is difficult to find even by Tokyo standards. But their famous ramen is so damn good that it is worth defying your social phobia, pressing a button on the ramen machine and taking a chance.

- Open Saturday to Wednesday 11.30am–3pm, 6.30–10pm
- Hatagaya
- 2-47-12 Hatagaya

Ginza Noodles Clam Ramen

Mussel ramen may sound like something you eat when you lose a bet, but don't let that scare you off. This Ginza shop has a broth consisting of no less than three broths: chicken, mussels and *niboshi* (dried sardines). Everything is held together by a *shoyu* that is deeper than a hungover Barry White. The other ingredients also reflect the best of "local" produce: the mussels are from the Kawana region, the noodles are made by an artisan in Kyoto and the eggs are said to be the best in Japan. They also serve a tsukemen (p. 20) and a very good *mazemen* – a dry kind of ramen without broth but with more options for additions.

- ⊙ Open Monday to Friday 11.30am–10pm, Saturday 11.30am–9pm
- ⓓ Ginza
- ⓐ 6-12-2 Ginza

HOW TO USE A RAMEN MACHINE

Don't let the screen scare you, it's easier than you think to order ramen in Tokyo, and many ramen machines have pictures, English text or helpful Japanese speakers nearby – and even if you don't fully understand what you ordered, that's just exciting. But if you are completely lost here is a guide for using the ramen machine.

1. CHOOSE YOUR RAMEN

You often start by ordering what type of ramen you want – some places only have one kind while others have several. Although ramen is a dish that can be varied indefinitely, there are four basic types, plus one where the noodles are dipped into the broth, which are available at most ramen restaurants. These are:

醤油ラーメン SHOYU RAMEN
Shoyu means soy and is a clear chicken or vegetable broth flavored with just soy.

塩ラーメン SHIO RAMEN
Shio means salt and is a light, clear salt-spiced broth cooked with chicken, fish or vegetables.

味噌ラーメン MISO RAMEN
Chicken or fish broth mixed with miso for a cloudy, nutty, sweet and salty soup. A personal favorite.

豚骨ラーメン TONKOTSU RAMEN
Ramen with a tasty, oily, cloudy and ridiculously good broth, cooked with, among other things, pork legs and pig feet.

つけ麺 TSUKEMEN
Ramen variant where the noodles are thicker and served alongside the tasty broth that you then dip them into.

2. CUSTOMISING YOUR RAMEN

Do you want extra spicy ramen, a larger portion or those thicker noodles that look so good on Instagram? You can request these additional options either on the machine or at the counter when handing over your ticket. Sometimes there are even small pieces of paper to fill in and sometimes the ramen chef asks you directly. In any case, here are some common choices:

大盛 OOMORI
>An extra large portion of ramen.

替え玉 KAE-DAMA
>An extra portion of noodles for leftover broth.

太い FUTOI
>Thick noodles.

細い HOSOI
>Thin noodles.

固め KATAME
>Al dente noodles.

辛い KARAI
>Extra spicy ramen.

こってり KOTTERI
>Extra thick broth.

油 ABURA
>Fat – some places add extra chicken fat.

3. CHOOSE YOUR TOPPINGS

It is the various toppings that really make a bowl of ramen, and even if some toppings are included, you can add extras. What is included, however, can be difficult to understand, so it is easy to double up. For example, I have often eaten ramen with two soy-marinated, perfectly cooked *onsen tamago* eggs. But as they say, when life gives you two soy-marinated, perfectly cooked *onsen tamago* eggs, eat both.

チャーシュー CHASHU
>Marinated, slow-cooked pork belly or other cut of pork.

玉子 TAMAGO
>Boiled eggs, usually perfectly creamy, sometimes marinated in soy.

海苔 NORI
>Dried seaweed.

ネギ NEGI
>Finely chopped spring onion.

もやし MOYASHI
>Bean sprouts, often flash-fried.

ごま GOMA
>Sesame seeds, either whole, ground or sesame oil.

にんにく NINNIKU
>Garlic, often freshly grated.

UDON, SOBA & TEMPURA

Thick wheat noodles, thin buckwheat noodles and battered and deep-fried vegetables and seafood

Eating in Tokyo is not just about filling up on ramen – Japan has many other types of noodles. There are plenty of different stories about how noodles originally came to Japan from China – all contain some kind of Zen monk. No matter which of them is true, it is a fact that medieval influencers have had a tremendous impact on Japanese food culture. From bringing back a variety of dishes from their travels in China and Korea, to how these were then prepared: thoughtfully, carefully, made-to-order. When the thick, wheat-based udon noodles first came to Japan, they were fancy upper-class

food, while the thinner, more slender buckwheat noodles, "soba", were simple food for the working class. So, exactly the opposite of how it is today.

Today, udon is Japan's answer to ham sandwiches – a satisfying filling food that is often served in simple fast food restaurants. Of course, this doesn't mean that the quality suffers. On the contrary, udon noodles are often hand cut at the restaurant, perfectly cooked and served with a simple broth so full of umami that you may suffer withdrawal symptoms for two weeks after you get home. Udon noodles can be served cold or hot, with dipping sauce or with everything from curry to the classic *kakejiru* – a simple noodle broth of soy sauce, dashi and mirin. Serving tempura on the side has almost become standard. The combination of soft noodles and crispy battered and deep-fried vegetables and seafood is quite spectacular. The latest noodle craze in Tokyo is called *sanuki* udon and is a variant derived from the "udon districts" in Kagawa. Japanese people travel to Kagawa from all over the country to eat udon. In Kagawa there are udon buses that take you on udon tours and udon taxis with udon bowls on the roof whose drivers know all the really good udon places.

This is also where *Udon* is set – a film about a failed comedian who mainly drifts around and eats udon. The film became a great success with both viewers and critics in Japan but did not do as well in the west. The *LA Times* wrote that the film contains "too much udon-eating" and that there was so much udon in this film that things like plot and character development were forgotten.

Soba noodles are both very similar to udon noodles and not. Just like udon, you can eat soba noodles cold or hot, with some kind of sauce or broth. At the same time, buckwheat is more expensive and more difficult to work with than ordinary wheat flour, which means that soba restaurants are often minimalistic and formal and the soba maker a serious artisan who, in some cases, will go as far in their quest for perfection as a sushi or *kaiseki* chef. The nutty taste of buckwheat is also subtle, so soba is often served very simply: just some gray, cold noodles in a bamboo dish with a small bowl of *kakejiru* on the side.

I really love the cold, chewy soba noodles, but they're not super filling, and don't expect any explosion of flavor, rather it's more like comfort food.

There are also a couple of little things to think about when eating soba. First of all, you should always taste the noodles and the broth before adding the extras – it is like tasting before you add salt. You don't bite off the noodles either; you should slurp them into your mouth, especially if they're hot. You can drink the broth straight from the bowl if you want, and if you dip your soba noodles, hold the dipping bowl near your mouth so you don't spill the broth. If you are eating tempura with the soba noodles, you shouldn't dip it in the *kakejiru* because when you've finished, a jug of buckwheat-tasting cooking water is served to pour into the dipping sauce, which is then eaten as a soup.

Shin Udon

If you want to eat high-quality *sanuki* udon from Kagawa, you have to take the subway to Shinjuku, walk a couple of blocks and start looking for a gathering of people with rumbling tummies in a quiet residential area. Shin has been considered one of the city's best udon places since they opened in 2009 and has as a consequence had an udon queue since then. But don't worry, it moves so much faster than a ramen queue for a restaurant of the same caliber. However, this does not mean that it is not as good.

Just like their Italian cousins, udon is much more about the noodles than the broth. And at Shin, the noodles are made from scratch and cooked to order. In a small room with street-facing windows, noodle master Shinji Narahara is rolling, cutting, boiling and cooling udon noodles. The result is both sophisticated and mind-blowing – a bit like having your "brains

smashed out with a slice of lemon wrapped round a large gold brick", as Douglas Adams wrote in *Hitchhikers Guide to the Galaxy*. The noodles are chewy, thick, slippery and completely addictive.

There are three basic variants on the menu: *kake* udon, which is hot noodles; *zaru* udon, which is cold noodles with a cold dipping sauce; or *bukkake* udon, which isn't what you think but cold noodles with "a splash" of cold dashi broth. These come with a variety of optional extras such as tempura, beef or salmon roe. Extremely good. Don't miss Shin's specialty, a carbonara-inspired udon with raw egg, parmesan, butter, black pepper and, listen up, a tempura-fried piece of bacon!

o Open Sunday to Thursday 11am–11pm, Friday and Saturday 11am–12am

d Shinjuku

a 2-20-16 Yoyogi

Oniyanma

Just outside Gotanda metro station is this cheap, sort of divey, wonderful little udon shop for budget-minded night owls and frugal early birds. The style here is *sanuki* udon with its wide, flat noodles, and you can get them in a hot broth or cold sauce, with exactly the kind of tempura you prefer. But whatever you choose, do it quickly; this is a teeny tiny place with a fast turnover and neither customers nor staff have time for indecision. Quickly select your udon on the machine – don't worry if you don't understand what it says, just pick something, everything is good and costs around 5 bucks. Display the tickets on your table, put your bag down and by the time you look up, a bowl of freshly made udon noodles with delicious tempura is in front of you. Slurp a noodle into your udon-hole and shed a tear over how good it is. Eat up and leave in the wink of an eye.

- Open Monday to Saturday 7am–3am, Sunday 7am–12am
- Gotanda
- 4-1-20 Higashishinagawa

Dosanjin

If ramen and udon are heavy, filling and fatty, then soba is light and wholesome. And you want that sometimes, right? If you are looking for a fresh noodle dish, there is none fresher than Dosanjin's famous *sudachi* soba, a modern Tokyo classic and beloved summer dish. It is cold, handmade soba noodles in a cold broth topped with thinly cut *sudachi* – a kind of lime-like Japanese citrus fruit. These citrus slices make the noodles taste incredibly fresh, a little like quenching your thirst in a crystal clear spring creek. If you want to increase the decadence, Dosanjin also has an extremely good, warm and umami-rich *ankake* soba and, of course, tempura.

But Dosanjin doesn't just have good food, it's got a nice atmosphere too – down a flight of stairs in a house beside the beautiful Meguro River in Nakameguro. It has its own small soba factory at the entrance and a Japanese stone garden to contemplate while slurping up your chewy noodles.

- Open every day except Monday 11.30am–3pm and 6–11pm
- Nakameguro
- 3-19-8 Aobadai

Soba Yakko

Are you an architect, gallery owner or possibly an art director with creative dreams and want to eat something that fits your minimalist lifestyle and matches your new Helmut Lang pants? Then you must visit the small, Michelin-BIB-listed neighborhood pub Soba Yakko. Here they serve soba noodles exactly how people in round bakelite glasses want them: handmade, nutty, chewy and very, very simple. Just a nice gray pile of noodles on a beautiful brown bamboo dish with a light dipping sauce on the side. And if you feel a bit wild, they also have good snacks and even *kakiage* – a magnificent tempura cake. Even the restaurant itself has a natural kind of elegance. It is not designed neatly, but feels more like it just became that way – a long wooden counter where devout soba lovers slurp up noodles in silence before they pay, bow and walk out.

- Open Tuesday to Sunday 5–10pm, Saturday 12–4pm
- Meguro
- 3-4-13 Takaban

Oniyanma

Soba Yakko

Dosanjin

Kaneko Hannosuke

Sometimes you just want to skip the noodles and go straight to the tempura. When it comes to tempura places, they span the whole spectrum: from simple, dingy deep-fried-smelling joints to fancy Michelin-star places with tasting menus. My absolute favorite style of tempura is somewhere in between. Kaneko Hannosuke is a real classic in Nihonbashi, named after its founder who as a child inherited the secret recipe for their famous tempura sauce. This place is extremely popular but you can't book a table. In fact, if the queues say anything about the food then Kaneko Hannosuke has Tokyo's best – they are said to consistently have the longest queues in the city. You may have to wait up to three hours, so get here early and bring a book or fully charged iPhone. In case of cold weather, the people lining up are offered steaming cups of *mugi-cha* – grain tea.

Extremely cozy, but still frustrating. When you finally enter the room, all the irritation drains away. This is the very definition of comfort food. Kaneko Hannosuke serves mainly two things. One is a so-called *edomae-tendon* – a tempura *donburi* that's a Tokyo classic. It consists of a bowl of rice topped with a bunch of perfectly fried shrimps, octopus, conger eel and a soft-boiled egg, and that secret sauce. If you sit at the long counter, you can also choose to eat *tempura-meshi*, which means a fixed menu consisting of rice, pickles, an absolutely fantastic miso soup and today's tempura bites, which are placed on your plate as they are cooked.

And all this for around US$10.

- ⊙ Open Monday to Friday 11am–10pm, Saturday and Sunday 10am–9pm
- ⓓ Nihonbashi
- ⓐ 1-4-3 Nihonbashi-Honcho

The market outside Nogi temple

—————— FACTS ——————

SHOPPING FOR FOOD LOVERS

Temple market   *Tsukiji*   *Kappabashi*

A Japanese chef's knife is at the top of the shopping list for many Tokyo travelers. My hottest tip is to find one of the markets that are held outside certain Buddhist temples almost every weekend. In addition to stylish *ukiyo-e* prints, indigo textiles and old porcelain, there is usually at least one stall that deals with antique, super beautiful carbon-steel knives. Google "temple market Tokyo".

If you still want to buy a new knife, or anything kitchen-related really, Kappabashi Kitchen Town is the place to go. It is an area entirely dedicated to kitchen equipment, and here you can find everything from coffee machines to plastic models of food. Kama-Asa is my personal favorite, and they have not only a separate knife section but also the best selection of table grills and binchotan (white) charcoal.

Tsukiji Outer Market also has a lot of shopping. Here you will find knife dealers, delicatessens and kitchen shops. But most are quite old school, so for something more modern, check out nearby Hitachiya.

Afterwards you have to buy lots of food to bring home from Japan. Why else did you bring two suitcases with you?

YAKINIKU

Wagyu, binchotan and the art of sharing a meal

Yakiniku is beef, usually wagyu, which is grilled in thinly cut bite-size pieces on a table grill. When the meat is ready, you stuff it into your mouth while simultaneously placing a new bite on the grill. Mix the meat up with rice, vegetables and other side dishes that sometimes have Korean origin – and sometimes not. For many Japanese, yakiniku is a Korean way of eating. For Koreans, however, it is Japanese. I would say that yakiniku is simply a Japanese version of Korean BBQ, which over time has evolved into its own style.

The reason for this combination is historic. From the Middle Ages onwards it was forbidden to eat meat in Japan. They ate fish, rice and pickles, but when Emperor Meiji – in an attempt to bring Japan closer to the rest of the world – abolished the meat ban in 1872, they could finally add 200 gram steak to the shopping list. However, the Japanese didn't really know how to prepare this new, exciting ingredient, so they turned to the Korean portion of the population, who had a longstanding high-quality BBQ culture with their *bulgogi*, *galbi* and *samgyupsal*, for advice. In this way Korean BBQ spread all over Japan and changed over time, becoming more Japanese, and before they knew it yakiniku was born. Today, the boundaries between what is yakiniku and what is Korean BBQ are still quite fluid.

But the most important thing to keep in mind is that yakiniku is the type of food you graze on. You share it with your friends over a long period of time, which can feel unfamiliar if you are accustomed to getting your own plate of food that you devour in five minutes. But soon you will realize how liberating it can be to open up to the company and literally *share* a meal with people you like. Talking about the food, ordering more short ribs and *zabuton*, recommending combinations, signaling for another beer, moaning loudly when you gobble up a particularly good piece of meat. It's actually the best thing ever.

Even though yakiniku is a collective way of cooking, one person usually has the main responsibility, and it is often the person who holds the BBQ tongs. This person moves cooked meat to a cooler spot on the grill, extinguishes flaring flames with an ice cube and makes sure to add fresh meat and more vegetables when they are needed.

Korean BBQ is eaten much like yakiniku with one big difference: you make small, *ssam* (wraps), with the meat before you stuff them in your mouth. Now, there is no right or wrong when you make a *ssam*. Some people just put a little meat in a salad leaf while others make loaded vegetable tacos with meat, rice, kimchi, *ssamjang* sauce and possibly double or triple wraps. Some people just dip the meat in a little sesame oil and eat the salad leaf like a rabbit afterwards. However, you always eat the entire wrap in a single bite; taking a small bite is considered strange.

Tokyo is full of delightful BBQ restaurants; you don't have to eat in a super fancy place but can get a fantastic experience by just stumbling in somewhere on a whim. The first thing I usually check is how popular the place appears to be. A queue is always a good sign, same with people waddling out of the restaurant with squinting eyes – that they have been there for a while = good. After that I check that they actually use coal in the grills and, if you are a little nerdy, what kind of coal. This says a lot about a restaurant. I also check what people are eating and how many side dishes there seems to be and how exciting they are, and what types of meat you can choose from. You want a good mix of cheap pork belly and expensive A5-wagyu for a perfect yakiniku experience.

Sumibi Yakiniku Nakahara

Don't come to Sumibi Yakiniku Nakahara and expect to find a vegetarian option. Because here you eat wagyu like sushi. The meat *shokunin* Kentaro Nakahara stands in the kitchen and cuts off the finest bite-sized pieces of beef from the districts of Matsusaka, Kobe or Omi, which are then served one by one in a dizzying BBQ *omakase*. There aren't many vegetables. There aren't many side dishes. And it's not cheap. But the thinly cut A5-steak that's just been coal-kissed on the grill can be the perfect bite of meat and a reason to become wagyu-tarian.

- **o** Open every day 5–11pm, reservations recommended
- **d** Chiyoda
- **a** Gems Ichigaya 9F, 4-3 Rokubancho

Yakinuku Kunimoto Shinkan

Before chefs like Kentaro Nakahara at
Sumibi Yakiniku Nakahara (p. 38) began
modernizing yakiniku, there were places
like this: simple but meticulous restaurants
somewhere between classic fine dining
and noisy neighborhood joints. Kunimoto
serves carefully selected *omakase* menus,
consisting of personally chosen cuts of beef,
cooked using charcoal of oak from Nagoya.
It is also a place where you can get a little
giggly from too many beers. Wonderful!

You can choose between three sizes of
menu – from around US$50 to US$100.
For each menu – served inside a stylish
box – there is a bunch of seasoned,
perfectly cut pieces of meat that you choose
from and grill yourself at the table. For
the really hungry there is also a menu for
about US$220.

But not all meat melts in the mouth at
Kunimoto. They have specialized in serving
meat that's a little leaner, and when it comes
to wagyu this is often a good thing. Many
of the best, most flavorsome pieces of meat
are actually a bit tougher, so don't get upset
if you are forced to chew.

The side dishes are simple and classic.
A couple of different kimchi varieties, a
good green salad with *goma dare* (Japanese
sesame sauce) and rice and cucumber with
miso dip.

Extremely simple yet so good.

- Open every day except Monday
  5–10pm/11pm, reservation recommended
- Hamamatsucho
- Kano Bldg 1F, 2-8-9 Hamamatsucho

Onoda Shoten

This small modern yakiniku bar in Nakameguro is one of the places that seems to be on the verge of not serving tourists. They believe that we (tourists) never show up for reservations, and we don't even like to BBQ *horumon* (intestines) but just want wagyu, wagyu, wagyu all the time. But if you come on time, are polite and happily gobble up tongue and intestine, it is the world's nicest, most hospitable place.

- Open every day except Tuesday 6pm–2am
- Nakameguro
- 3-7-3 Kamimeguro

Jiromaru

As soon as I land in Tokyo, I usually go directly to Jiromaru in Shinjuku: a small, almost 24-hour yakiniku place where you stand by a counter, choose a couple pieces of meat, some side dishes and then grill it all yourself on a gas BBQ. I know it goes against my "only binchotan charcoal" rule but Jiromaru is so good and simple that it works anyway – you are in and out in half an hour if you want. The world's best fast food. Jiromaru doesn't have an English menu, instead, the day's specials are written on wooden signs on the walls with the price per item underneath. It's cheap, despite the high-quality meat from the Shiga and Nagano districts. If you feel uncertain, you can always point to features that are displayed in the counter (like at a sushi restaurant), ask them to recommend something or just try and order anyway.

Why not start with a piece of *gyutan* (beef tongue)? It is cheap but good BBQ food and has some of the same characteristics as wagyu. Extremely good. *Karubi* means short ribs and is a fantastic, slightly more filling classic that is cut into thicker slices, up to ⅓ inch (1 cm). *Zabuton* is a small steak that is cut from the upper portion of the chuck, and it's extremely good. I know that we make stew with chuck steak in Sweden, but in Japan it is one of the most sought after pieces because of its taste, texture and because there isn't much of it on the cow.

To finish, you point to one of the signs furthest away that are marked "A5" and have a higher price than the others. These are the most expensive, most marbled pieces of beef and entrecote that are often sliced wafer-thin and grilled quickly. Let them just touch the grill, stuff them in your mouth, close your eyes to savor the moment and continue with your day.

o Open every day except Sunday
11.30am–5am

d Shinjuku

a 1-26-3 Kabukicho

Honke Ponga

If the boundaries between yakiniku and Korean BBQ are fluid, Honke Ponga is definitely closer to the latter. It's a simple, inexpensive, relaxed place with a patio covered with plastic tarpaulins – a bit like a Korean *pojangmacha*. You put the meat in the *ssam* (wraps) and drink whole bottles of *soju* with the food. It has a young crowd, mostly couples on dates and groups of friends who literally stumble out of the restaurant after a couple of hours of too much beer and too little oxygen.

It's the kind of simple, but extremely good, BBQ joint that are everywhere in Tokyo, except for one thing: Honke Ponga has a larger vegetable selection than most other similar restaurants. They have several kinds of kimchi, a variety of Korean *banchans* (side dishes) and you can order a dish of 15 different types of Korean *sangchu* salad to wrap around your grilled meat. Wonderful. Because all the chefs are Korean, you can also get good stuff like *gomguk* (a rich meaty soup), Korean noodles and various kinds of stews.

- **o** Open every day 5–11pm
- **d** Meguro
- **a** 2-17-5 Kami-Osaki

43

Niku Yokocho

Despite the name, Niku Yokocho is not in an alley but is a large newly built foodcourt with 25 BBQ joints found on the second and third floors above a department store in the middle of tourist-packed Shibuya. It's pretty handy being able to just drop in if you're staying in any of the hotels nearby. Here you can find everything from yakiniku and Korean BBQ to yakitori places and some *horumonyaki*.

All equally messy, but fun.

The meat quality is so-so, the BBQs are powered by liquid gas, tables and chairs are made from old beer crates. It's open until 5am and the customers consist mostly of highly intoxicated young people – once

I saw, for the first time ever in East Asia, a fight in the alley outside. I was as surprised as the police, who didn't really seem to know how to handle the situation.

In many ways, Niku Yokocho is the Japanese equivalent of a late night diner in a small town. With one big difference: the food here is incredibly good.

ⓞ Open every day except Sunday 5pm–5am
ⓓ Shibuya
ⓐ Chitose Kaikan 2–3F

FACTS

KOREAN BBQ IN SHIN-OKUBO

At Korean BBQ places in Japan you can usually get wagyu, but they also grill simpler, cheaper meat pieces like *galbi* (short ribs) and *samgyupsal* (pork belly). There is a greater focus on kimchi and different kinds of *banchans*, and they are louder, more lively places; somewhere you go to have fun with friends rather than for a great culinary experience.

The largest concentration of Korean BBQ is around Shin-Okubo station. The area was the cheapest in Tokyo for a long time, which meant that the Korean laborers who were forced to go to Japan under the colonial rule settled here. Today, it is Japan's largest Korea Town with long rows of Korean restaurants, supermarkets and convenience stores selling honey-butter chips, Shin Ramyun instant noodles and four-liter soy sauce bottles. Here you'll find Korean pop culture, Korean make-up and super-styled Korean K-pop artists distributing flyers and showing off while waiting to break through in Japan. The area has unfortunately also been prone to a lot of violence and anti-Korean demonstrations by Japanese nationalists, who don't recognize how much of their culture really comes from their neighboring country to the west.

YAKITORI & YAKITON

Chicken and meat on skewers, grilled over glowing charcoal

Before the Japanese meat ban was lifted in the late 1800s, people sometimes cheated and ate meat that was in the "gray area". They ate poultry, birds and small game, and wild boar was referred to as mountain whale to avoid a guilty conscience.

Mostly, however, they ate retired fighting roosters, generally of the Thai breed shamo. The roosters were leaner, sinewy and chewier than the chickens we are accustomed to, and even today it is often shamo that is served at exclusive yakitori places. However, the smell of grilled meat was considered vulgar(!), so they ate them in the form of *shamo-nabe*, a slow-cooked fighting-rooster stew. Moreover, *shamo-nabe* is said to have been the legendary police samurai Hasegawa Heizo's favorite dish. He was a tough man who led a special force of reformed criminals to clean up Edo's underworld. He didn't always follow the rules, but he certainly got results!

When the meat ban was finally lifted, the Japanese were naturally hungry for chicken. It was considered more exclusive than both pork and beef, and only the fanciest restaurants could afford to buy it. Enterprising street-food chefs raided the garbage of these places, and soon they started grilling stuff like chicken rump, skin and breast cartilage.

And it was ridiculously good. People went crazy over this new dish – yakitori. Even today, it is common to literally eat the whole chicken, and there are plenty of restaurants purely for so-called *horumon* – grilled "thrown away pieces". When you grill pork the same way as yakitori it is called yakiton, and *kushiyaki* is a broad term for grilled food on sticks.

Today, people are just as happy eating yakitori standing under a subway track as they are eating it as part of a tasting menu at a fancy Michelin-star restaurant. But regardless of where you eat yakitori, it is always the same dish that is served: chicken on skewers, grilled over glowing high-quality coal, either dipped in a BBQ sauce or smeared with salt. It's really that simple. And difficult. Yakitori is nothing special while at the same time it is the best thing in the whole world.

Even though yakitori is available everywhere, from izakayas to your local convenience store, it is a quintessential Tokyo experience to eat in a dedicated yakitori place where grazing has become an art form and an all-evening activity. You can indeed order a *yakitori moriawase* (a plate of mixed skewers), but the real pleasure lies in ordering the skewers one by one, when you crave them, while you drink beer and talk shit.

Kushiwakamaru

For traditional, old-school yakitori, a visit to Kushiwakamaru in Nakameguro is recommended. It is a smoky, loud, simple neighborhood pub with low prices, fast service, lots of noise, cold beer and exceptionally good charcoal-grilled chicken. The atmosphere is brusque but nice, the place crowded but cheerful. It can be argued that there are thousands of restaurants like this in Tokyo, and that is actually true. Kushiwakamaru is a quite common yakitori pub – just a little better.

The Nakameguro district is generally known for yakitori. Several of the city's most flashy places like **Torishiki** and **Toriyoshi** are located here. But they are expensive and impossible to get a table at, while Kushiwakamaru is just about having fun. The queues can be long, however, so come early or call between 1pm and 5pm to book a table for the same day.

- Open every day 5pm–12am
- Nakameguro
- 1-19-2 Kamimeguro

Fuku Yakitori

If Kushiwakamaru represents a traditional yakitori pub, Fuku in Yoyogi-Uehara is an example of a slightly more modern place. It has a stylish interior and even serves craft beer. Fuku is also a good compromise for those who want to eat quality yakitori without sacrificing the nice neighborhood pub atmosphere by booking a table at a stuffy Michelin yakitori place. Honestly, Fuku's yakitori is better than some of the Michelin-star restaurants because they don't serve the expensive yet tough shamo chicken, but high-quality jidori chicken, which could be described as the chicken equivalent of wagyu: a free-range, small-scale bred chicken known for its good taste, as well as being able to be eaten raw in the form of sashimi.

As in most yakitori places, a skewer costs around US$3 each, but you can eat many. And when you get tired of chicken, there are also various beef, pork and seafood skewers to mix it up. Happily, Fuku also has a large section of bacon-wrapped options. For example, what about bacon-wrapped mushrooms and asparagus, or my favorite, grilled shishito peppers stuffed with processed cheese?

- **o** Open every day except Wednesday 5.30–11.30pm
- **d** Yoyogi
- **a** 3-23-4 Nishihara

Akira Nakameguro

Akira Nakameguro

Akira Nakameguro

If you visit Tokyo during cherry blossom season, I cannot think of a better restaurant than Akira. It is located in an extremely beautiful place along the Meguro River's avenue of cherry trees, and during *sakura* season (cherry blossom season) the restaurant's facade is opened up so that the entire restaurant overflows with the bittersweet reminder of the fleetingness of beauty and the relentless cycle of life.

Of course, Akira is also nice during other seasons, although be prepared: here you sit on tatami mats on the floor and eat mostly chicken intestines. So Akira is not a traditional yakitori restaurant, instead you could describe it as a chicken *horumonyaki* – where "*yaki*" means "grilled" and "*horumon*" means "thrown-away bits". They serve the stuff ordinary restaurants don't want. True nose-to-tail you could call it. In an incredibly fancy wooden box, you are presented with stuff like gizzard, rump, heart, neck, ribs and breast cartilage to cook yourself on a small table grill. Everything, except maybe the gizzard, is actually fantastic and something of an experience. If you are really adventurous, you can even eat chicken sashimi – one of Tokyo's best, according to experts.

For more traditional palates, regular chicken is also available, and the *tsukune* is especially delicious: a juicy chicken meatball, wrapped in *shiso* and grilled, and then dipped in a poached egg. Wonderful.

Akira is a popular place amongst the locals in Nakameguro, so call ahead to book a table or drop in and check if there is any availability later in the week.

- Open every day 5pm–2am
- Nakameguro
- Riverside Terrace 106 1-10-23 Nakameguro

Saitamaya

Saitamaya in Jujo is a simple neighborhood pub where people in the area go to become saloon-drunk, but where the food is of fine-dining quality and where you can get a close to perfect Tokyo experience; at least if you follow a couple of simple rules. They are: cash only, no photography, no playing with your cellphone and no table booking. You must obediently wait your turn. So show up early!

You can't order soft drinks or water either, or have any special requests whatsoever. Instead you politely drink either ice-cold beer or *shochu* sours, which are amazingly good and consist of frozen, slushy, cheap *shochu* that is shaken out of magnum bottles into highball glasses that are then filled with lemon soda. Don't be foolish and not finish all the nine wonderful yakiton skewers you get served from the fixed menu, whether they are black Jeju pig and wagyu or guts and kidney. Whatever they serve, I promise that it will taste amazing. Here is a genuine BBQ *shokunin* at work.

If you can follow Saitamaya's rather strict rules and get a seat at the bar, I promise that you will get not only a warm welcome but also get to witness a showman and master chef handling the BBQ like a yakiton-Elvis. It is amazing to see, kind of like Anthony Bourdain serving gourmet food at Burger King. It seems so simple. Until an apprentice takes over, and, in a couple of seconds, the sole tiny yakitori grill turns into a burning inferno.

- Open every day except Sunday 4–9.30pm
- Jujo
- 2-5-12 Higashi-Jujo

Memory Lane aka Piss Alley

Bad yakitori is not the worst. And nowhere else do they have better bad yakitori than in Omoide Yokocho aka Memory Lane aka Piss Alley. The narrow alleyway in the middle of modern Shinjuku does not, however, smell at all like piss, but more of BBQ, due to all the yakitori places that are gathered here. Piss Alley has indeed become something of a tourist destination in recent years but is still quite adorable.

ⓘ Most of the places are open in the evening till late

ⓓ Shinjuku

ⓐ 1-2-8 Nishi-Shinjuku

HOW TO EAT YAKITORI

It is not much harder to eat yakitori than to buy loose candy – you just choose what you want, when you want it. There are a few little things to consider. First of all, you usually eat the skewer that is salted first, because they are more subtle in taste than those with *tare* (Japanese dipping sauce) or BBQ sauce. You also always eat the chicken straight off the skewer; there's usually a jar on the table where you put the used skewers (see picture). There are usually also condiments such as *shichimi togarashi* – a chili mixture you can use for seasoning if you want. If the yakitori restaurant has an *omakase* menu, you don't have to choose at all – just make an effort to taste everything – otherwise you should eat yakitori in the following order:

1. Start with *toriniku* (chicken breast). Then try the classic *negima* (thighs with spring onions). Good.

2. For sides, order *kawa* (crispy skin) and *tebasaki* (chicken wings). Two really crispy favorites.

3. Mix it up with grilled vegetables and skewers like ginkgo nuts, shishito, grilled chili or shiitake.

4. Now it's time for a mighty *tsukune* (chicken meatball), which you dip into egg yolk. Astonishingly good.

5. Order your favorites on replay or try other options like rump or *uzura no tamago* (grilled quail eggs).

6. Finish with a *yaki onigiri* (grilled rice ball) or *oyakodon* (a rice bowl with grilled chicken and egg).

JAPANESE CURRY

Adopted home cooking and comfort food

Japanese food is associated with things like sushi, tempura and yakiniku. But it's possible the most popular dish of them all is curry. Yes, you read correctly, the Japanese version of Indian curry has, for practical reasons and historical coincidence, become somewhat of a national dish in Japan.

When Japanese children vote on their favorite school lunch, it is curry that tops the list year after year. When you want to cook something fast, simple and warming at home, you make curry. On every street corner in Japan you can find places that offer *kare raisu* (curry and rice), curry udon, curry *tonkatsu* or curry buns. Even though curry comes from India, it is a dish that, like Chinese noodles, has spread throughout the world and taken a variety of forms. Today, there are famous local curries everywhere from Thailand and Malaysia to

Ethiopia and Jamaica – all equally different and delicious.

Curries have most often found their new homelands via trade routes, labor migration or the waves of imperialism – but Japan's love of curry did not emerge in any of these ways. Instead, it is said to have been British sailors who brought it with them when Japan opened up to the world during the Meiji restoration in the late 1800s.

So you could say that Japanese curry has more in common with a British curry than a genuine Indian curry. That has since become even more Japanified. It is soft, mild and comforting, and is served with short-grain rice and Japanese pickles. It is also made with a base of so-called curry roux – a kind of curry block that you break into pieces and add to the pot. These curry blocks are sold as partially cooked products and are considered to be another reason for the dish's popularity: unlike other Japanese cooking, curry is not surrounded by a lot of traditions, complicated cooking methods and pretentious food craftsmen and *shokunin*.

No disrespect to sushi, tempura and yakiniku, but sometimes you just want to cook something fast, pour a ladle of brown, spicy sauce over a bit of tasty rice and eat it with a spoon in front of a TV show where a Japanese celebrity in diapers is trying to eat noodles in a dryer. In short, Japanese curry is simply practical comfort food

and adopted home cooking – a bit like spaghetti with meat sauce is to most of the western world.

Curry, however, is not just popular, it can be hip, too. A younger generation of foodies has rediscovered the dish, and it is a common topic in everything from Japanese song lyrics and TV series to curry blogs and manga series. The clothing brand A Bathing Ape's founder Nigo has opened a curry shop in Harajuku in collaboration with Pharrell Williams, and the progressive Japanese food magazine *Rice*, devoted a whole issue to the dish.

Together with ramen, curry is also the dish that most often becomes a lifestyle for its fans. You discuss cooking methods, curry variants, favorite restaurants and, just like you can study judo, kendo and bushido, it is even said that you can study

curry-do – the way of curry. Young curry chefs even skip the curry-roux blocks and put at least as much effort into their spice mixtures as a ramen place does with their broth, and it has even become common for the curry to be genuinely Indian, Ethiopian or Thai. In Jinbocho, the district with the most curry places per capita in all of Japan, there is even a place that serves "European" curry, whatever that means. Boiled chicken in yellow curry with Uncle Ben's rice?

Maybe the memories of this kind of school-lunch curry are the reason it took me quite some time before I tried the Japanese variety. Today, however, I am a fully-fledged Japanese-curry nerd, highly addicted and excitedly studying curry-do.

After reading the following pages, you might become the same.

Land Curry & Coffee

If you are only planning a single curry meal during your visit to Tokyo, then enter Land Curry & Coffee in Meguro into Google Maps. In the stylish diner-like room, traditional Japanese curry is served – complete with unusual toppings such as processed cheese, poached eggs and mashed potatoes – but in an upgraded, modern way. In many ways, the curry at Land has more in common with a carefully balanced bowl of ramen than a chicken tikka at the local Indian restaurant. First, a spoonful of the sublime curry; whether you order a vegetarian curry, a classic chicken curry or a more experimental curry with shrimp and avocado, it's got depth and a perfectly balanced composition – you taste every individual spice. Absolutely wonderful. On the side: a dollop of creamy mashed potatoes to lessen the heat and a pile of short-grain rice, carefully formed into a

beautiful Mount Fuji. If you want eggs or processed cheese it is extra.

The concentration when the curry chefs grate nutmeg and sprinkle your curry with a little extra garam masala, black pepper, cumin seeds, finely chopped brown onion and a small blob of yuzu chili paste is fascinating and beautiful to see, so be sure to take a seat at the counter.

For dessert or as a drink with the meal: a sweet, spicy and very good chai tea.

- ⏰ Open Thursday and Friday 12–3.30pm, Saturday and Sunday 12–8pm
- 🚉 Meguro
- 📍 2F, 2-21-28 Shimomeguro

Hatos Outside

Hatos Outside

Hatos Outside is the curry version of the popular American BBQ pub Hatos Bar in Nakameguro, and, just like its cousin, here you get delicious food and ice-cold craft beer.

Here, the short-grain rice is shaped into a beautiful little mound covering the plate, and the day's rich, spicy curry dishes are served in small bowls. The finely chopped, Japanese pickles in yellow, green and pink are a nice touch, and together with an ice-cold Gigantic it is difficult not to get lots of warm fuzzy feelings. And while you're in the area, be sure to visit the Gotokuji Temple where the adorable waving cat, that has come to symbolize Tokyo, originates from.

- ◉ Open Tuesday to Friday 12–3pm and 6pm–12am, Saturday 12pm–12am, Sunday 12–10pm
- ⓓ Setagaya
- ⓐ Akamatsu Building, 4-22-5 Setagaya

Curry Kusamakura

This little curry shop in Shinjuku is a classic amongst Tokyo's curry nerds, so be prepared to line up along the narrow staircase that leads up to the restaurant on the second floor, especially if you arrive at lunchtime. The interior feels like a bohemian student pad: simple, homemade plywood furniture is crammed in with some Indian souvenir elephants, with staff that all look like they're studying a masters degree in curry. The curry at Kusamakura is not classic Japanese but inspired by the owner's backpacking trips to East Africa, Nepal and India. First of all, you get to choose the level of heat yourself. It is done on a scale from 1 to 10, where three is considered medium spicy and over five is ridiculously spicy – although a ten in Japan probably corresponds to a three in India.

- ◉ Open every day 11.30am–3pm and 6–9pm
- ⓓ Shinjuku
- ⓐ 2-4-9-2F Shinjuku

HOW TO MAKE JAPANESE CURRY

For the best possible curry, naturally, you make the spice mix from scratch. For a Japanese homemade curry, you use a so-called curry roux – a partially cooked curry in block form. It is available from mild to hot, although all of them are quite mild. A common brand is Golden Curry, which you will find in most Asian food stores.

INGREDIENTS, SERVES 4

cooking oil, for frying
2 brown onions, finely sliced
1 lb 2 oz (500 g) chicken, cut into
  bite-size pieces
2 carrots, cut into pieces
2 potatoes, cut into pieces
34 fl oz (1 L) chicken stock
1 tablespoon honey
2 tablespoons Japanese soy sauce
1 nashi pear or apple, grated
2 garlic cloves
2 inches (5 cm) piece of ginger
1 oz (25 g) Japanese curry roux

1. Heat some oil in a deep pot. Fry the onion and chicken until they start to color. Add the carrot and potato. Season with salt.

2. Add the stock, honey and soy sauce to the pot. Stir. Then add the pear, garlic and ginger.

3. Bring to the boil, lower the heat and simmer for about 1 hour. Skim off any impurities that rise to the surface, if necessary.

4. Add the curry roux to the pot and bring back to the boil. Lower the heat and simmer until the sauce thickens and becomes glossy.

5. Serve on a regular plate with freshly cooked short-grain rice on one side and curry on the other, garnish with Japanese pickles (optional). Eat with a spoon for maximum comfort.

CURRY & LITERATURE IN JINBOCHO

Japanese literature is often characterized by a bittersweet tone called *mono no aware*, which is the tender sorrow one might feel while experiencing the passage of time and the transience of things. Even though *mono no aware* is closely related to the western concept of nostalgia, it is not the same thing. Instead of a longing for an idealized past, it is about – in the spirit of true Zen Buddhism – a kind of melancholy presence in what is, but which will inevitably change, like that feeling you can get the last night of a trip, or when you look at your sleeping child and you're struck by how soon she will grow up.

Beauty and sorrow are often intertwined in Japanese literature, and if you, like me, enjoy it almost as much as curry, a visit to the Jinbocho district is recommended.

Jinbocho is Japan's literary center and is said to be the world's largest area for used books. In addition to being full of publishing houses, literary companies and used book shops, Jinbocho is also within walking distance of a handful of universities, which means the area is also full of cheap curry places. In fact, there are so many curry restaurants that the area alternately goes by the names "book town" and "curry town". Every year, a competition called Kanda Curry Grand Prix is held, where the top 20 curry places are chosen and the public competes over who can eat at the most restaurants.

Ethiopia, Bondy and Dylan are examples of classic curry pubs in Jinbocho, and even though the food in these places is quite simple, the experience of strolling around the area is pure *mono no aware*. You almost can't avoid feeling like a scruffy character from a Banana Yoshimoto novel when you read away an afternoon in a smoky cafe, browse through some books in a dusty used book store or settle down to dig into some cheap curry and contemplate the inevitable transience of things.

THREE NOVELS TO READ WHILE
EATING CURRY IN JINBOCHO

1. *Kitchen* by Banana Yoshimoto
2. *Norwegian Wood* by Haruki Murakami
3. *The Remains of the Day* by
   Kazuo Ishiguro

Curry bun from Temmaya

Temmaya

A curry bun tastes much like a salty donut with hot curry filling – it's incredibly good. After my latest Tokyo trip, it was neither sashimi nor ramen I was craving; it was curry buns! The original is said to have been invented at the bakery **Cattlea** in Morishita, but if you think that curry buns are your thing, instead I'd recommend a visit to the backpacker area Shimokitazawa, where there are plenty of simple bars, cheap fast food and small, cozy curry-bun bakeries. Be mindful of not just picking up a couple of buns with your hands – in Japanese bakeries you always take a tray to put your selected baked goods on.

A classic place in Shimokitazawa was until very recently the 50-year-old, quaint Angelica Bakery, which looked like a place that a Japanese Nina George could write feel-good novels about: *The Little Curry Bun Bakery in Shimokitazawa*. In addition to one of Tokyo's most famous curry buns, they also had the Japanese ninja action writer Shotaro Ikenami's favorite bun: miso bun or miso pan.

Just a curry-bun throw away from the former site of Angelica Bakery is Temmaya, which is actually a pretty unappealing curry restaurant but with one redeeming feature: from a small street restaurant they serve lovely, freshly deep-fried curry buns, perfectly soft and still warm. I am sorry, all bakery romantics, but unfortunately it beats freshly baked buns no matter how cozy the bakery is. This has made Temmaya extremely popular; they bake 600–700 curry buns a day and have a variety of options. My favorite is the one with a perfectly soft-boiled egg in the middle. When you bite into one of these, you immediately understand why curry buns are such a popular snack that they even have their own manga character. Karepanman (the curry-bun man) is a cousin of Anpanman (the bean-bun man) and has a bun for a head from where he sprays hot curry filling in the eyes of his enemies. Ouch!

- Open every day 11am–11.30pm
- Shimokitazawa
- 2F Kuwata Building, 2-12-12 Kitazawa

GYOZA & BIRU

The world's best food pairing

Vodka and caviar, sauternes and foie gras, Champagne and potato chips. Yes, there are many classic food pairings, but the question is whether the best of them all isn't gyoza and *biru* (beer). Nowadays in Tokyo, places have even started to serve gyoza with Champagne, craft beer or natural wine – but in my opinion, nothing beats a crisp, juicy Japanese dumpling and an ice-cold draft beer. Now, I know of course that craft-beer intellectuals think that Japanese lager tastes like malted Evian, but I find it to be such a sublime experience. Like so many other very simple things, the Japanese also think that a pint is worth doing very well. Japanese draft beer is poured out of high-tech space machines that: keep the beer so cold that you risk cracking your teeth, make a perfect head of foam and produce a lot of really small, carbon dioxide bubbles. There are machines that pour zero-degree Celsius (32 degrees Fahrenheit) beer, and

others that fill the glasses from the bottom and create a spinning tornado effect. There are machines that pour beer with a frozen slushie-like foam head, and there are machines that completely eliminate the human factor and are fully robotized.

The same philosophy cannot be said to apply to the humble gyoza. Where China is said to have 36 basic dumplings, Japan is content with the one. Which they do really damn well. Perfectly, I would almost dare say.

Gyoza is the direct Japanese translation of *jiaozi*, which is the Chinese name for dumplings. Legend has it that it was the father of Chinese herbal medicine Zhang Zhongjing who invented the dish 2,000 years ago as a remedy for people with cold ears – hence its characteristic ear shape. Although there were probably dumplings in Japan before this, this delicacy really took off in Japan when Japan invaded China in 1937 in a series of horrific events that preceded WWII.

Japanese soldiers stationed in northern China during the coming world war learned to both eat and cook Chinese *jiaozi*, recipes that they later brought home and began to adapt to Japanese taste. From the beginning, gyoza was mostly served as a complement to ramen, they both share a Chinese origin. Today, however, it is also a regular dish at izakayas, trendy bars and, of course, at dedicated gyoza restaurants.

Now, don't say you don't learn anything from eating gyoza and drinking biru!

The Japanese gyoza is smaller than its Chinese cousin and has a thinner, often factory-made, dough or wrapper. In the one basic gyoza, the filling consists of pork mince, ginger, garlic, cabbage and spring onion – although, of course, there are also variants with stuff like finely chopped shrimp, tofu, *uni* (sea urchin) and even processed cheese and pico de gallo (p. 79).

When you say "gyoza", you actually mean *yaki* gyoza, which is the most common variant and is cooked like a Chinese potsticker: the dumpling is fried in oil on a griddle or in a frying pan, water is poured over it and everything is covered with a lid, so the dumpling is steamed and fried at the same time, which gives a devilishly crisp underside and a heavenly smooth, soft top. Pretty brilliant really. *Sui* gyoza is dumplings in broth, *age* gyoza is a deep-fried gyoza and *mushi* gyoza is a steamed variant.

You never order a single gyoza but often at least six at a time, which usually stick together because of starch that leaks out. So, when you get your plate, gently separate a dumpling with your chopsticks and dip it into the small bowl where you made your own sauce by mixing equal parts soy sauce and vinegar from the bottles on the table, and season to taste with *rayu* – Japanese chili oil. If there is sesame oil, that is also good.

Wait a few seconds so your dumpling can cool a little, then stuff it in your mouth whole because you never take a bite of a gyoza. Then the juicy filling bursts out. Chew, swallow, take a sip of zero-degree Celsius (32 degrees Farenheit) biru and sigh like a city-dweller in an Akira Kurosawa movie: "*Aaaahhhhhh*".

Harajuku Gyoza Ro

Not far from the Harajuku places that sell rainbow cotton candy, half-meter fries and soft serve ice-cream in crepe cones, this dilapidated, old dive is located. And thank goodness for that, I don't know how you would manage to shop for Totoro figurines for the kids at Kiddyland without it. Harajuku Gyoza Ro is an institution that sells thousands of amazing gyoza at rocket speed from lunch to early morning daily. Sometimes there's a bit of a queue, but it moves fast. The speed is probably also helped by the fact that there are only two types of gyoza on the menu, fried or steamed; and three simple sides: cucumber with miso dip, pickled cabbage and bean sprouts with meat sauce. The gyoza costs about US$2 for six pieces and the side dishes about US$1.5, so you can afford to order everything, plus one or three biru.

- ⊙ Open Monday to Saturday 11.30am–4.30am, Sunday 11.30am–10pm
- ⓓ Harajuku
- ⓐ 6-2-4 Jingumae

Gyoza no Yasubei

If I had to choose a restaurant that really sums up what I love about Tokyo, it would be this little gyoza pub in Ebisu. It is not an expensive sushi place where it is impossible for mere mortals to get a table. It is not a modern, painfully hip pub. Instead, it's a simple, inexpensive, old-fashioned place where people go for a couple of ice-cold biru after work, but at the same time the food is of such good quality, and served at a pace even a Michelin-star restaurant couldn't achieve.

Early in the evening, there's already a long, snaking queue outside. When you finally enter the smoky premises, it is like you've entered a time machine and come out in Showa-era Tokyo (1926–89): there are red lanterns everywhere, old posters and photos, handwritten signs and rickety, playhouse-size tables and chairs. As a medium tall, somewhat chubby and very clumsy Swede, trying to settle down at the miniscule bar feels like you are Godzilla demolishing a small Japanese fishing village.

But everything is ok when the gyoza and biru are served.

The gyoza they serve originate from the Kochi prefecture in southern Japan. The filling is pretty standard: minced pork, ginger, garlic, cabbage, spring onion. What makes them so special is the specially made, paper-thin gyoza wrapper and that the gyoza are made and cooked to order. If you get a seat at the bar, you can see a genuine *shokunin* in action – at rocket speed and at hot-dog stand prices. After being masterfully made, the gyoza is steamed in *dashi* and fried in oil. The result is a dumpling so thin, delicate and crispy that it virtually melts in your mouth. It's like eating small umami hand grenades. They are also admirably small and so light that a small child could easily eat a portion of seven, so count on many extra orders.

- Open every day 5.30pm–3am
- Ebisu
- Hagiwara Building 5 1F, 4-9-15 Ebisu

Ohka the Best Days

The combination of gyoza and biru is awfully good, partly because for most people roughly 95 percent of their happy beer memories have been with a simple pint. I love a hop-rich IPA as much as anyone. I refuse to choose sides in the drink war. I am a fan of both craft beer and generic beer, natural wine and Bordeaux, craft bourbon and cheap whiskey. I drink everything as long as it's cold. So if you prefer to eat your gyoza with an Amarillo hops rauchbock in a pint glass with Big Bird from *Sesame Street* on the label, I don't judge you but instead recommend a visit to Ohka the Best Days in Nakameguro.

Ohka the Best Days may not have the best gyoza or the biggest beer selection – only six varieties on tap. But it is laidback, fun and has that wonderfully inclusive hipster hospitality. A large *ET* doll sits on a bicycle, the doorframe is full of punk stickers and in the corner there's an old TV showing old snowboard movies on VHS. The decor looks to be done by Brad Pitt's character in *True Romance*. And I think he would have liked the food: the gyoza is both homemade, crossover Mexican and stoner friendly. They are filled with processed cheese and topped with hot salsa and fresh coriander. Yes, I lied a little before. I love Ohka's gyoza. They taste like eating dumplings and tacos at the same time, and on the page opposite you can see how to make them at home (sort of).

- **o** Open every day except Sunday 6.30pm–12am
- **d** Nakameguro
- **a** Higashiyama, 2-4-8 Meguro-Ku

HOW TO MAKE OHKA'S GYOZA (SORT OF)

Japanese/Mexican crossover is not very common but works surprisingly well. For more traditional gyoza, just leave out the mozzarella and pico de gallo.

INGREDIENTS, MAKES 24 GYOZA

Filling
4 oz (100 g) white or pointed cabbage
1 spring onion
1 garlic clove
½ inch (approx.1 cm) ginger, peeled
2 teaspoons mirin
2 teaspoons Japanese soy sauce
2 teaspoons sesame oil
pinch of salt
4 oz (100 g) mozzarella, grated
7 oz (200 g) pork mince

24 gyoza wrappers
oil for frying

Pico De Gallo
9 oz (250 g) cherry tomatoes,
 finely chopped
½ white onion, finely chopped
1–2 jalapeños, finely chopped
fresh coriander, chopped
juice of ½ lime
salt

Dip
1 tablespoon Japanese soy sauce
1 tablespoon rice wine vinegar
1 tablespoon sesame oil
rayu (chili oil), to taste

1. Place the cabbage, spring onion, garlic and ginger in a food processor and finely chop, or you can of chop them by hand. Add the mirin, soy sauce, sesame oil, salt, mozzarella and pork mince and mix until well combined.

2. Make the pico de gallo by mixing the tomato, white onion, jalapeño and coriander in a bowl. Squeeze the lime juice over the top and season with salt.

3. Take the wrapper and place it in your palm. Put a little filling in the middle and then dip your finger in water and run it along the outer edge of half of the wrapper. Fold the wrapper in half to form a crescent moon and squeeze the edges together neatly, to get all of the air out. Prepare the rest of your gyoza. They can be frozen at this stage, but when cooking them from frozen, extend the steaming time.

4. Pour a little oil into a frying pan over medium heat. Once the oil is hot, add your gyoza and fry for about 5 minutes, until they start to get crunchy on the bottom. Then pour 2fl oz (50mL) water into the pan, cover with a lid and steam for about 3 minutes. Remove the lid and allow the water to boil off.

5. To make the dip, combine all the ingredients in a bowl and mix well.

6. Serve the gyoza crispy-side up, top with the pico de gallo and the dip on the side.

TONKATSU

Wiener schnitzel for connoisseurs

Tonkatsu is simple fast food and addictive deep-fried comfort food. But sometimes when you stuff the juicy, crispy pieces of pork in your mouth you can't help but feel that they are also something more. For instance, they make me think about sponge cake.

Let me explain. As I see it, there are two ways to think about sponge cake. One way is to think that sponge cake doesn't taste like much; that it is actually a rather boring cake and that you therefore have to spruce it up. So to make the sponge cake sweeter, you add a little vanilla sauce or whipped cream; for a little acidity, add a lot of fresh berries. All the initial problems with the concept of sponge cake are now solved, but at the same time it's no longer a sponge cake. Instead it is a cake.

So sometimes you could actually think the other way around. Instead of trying to figure out how to change the sponge cake, you ask the question: what is actually good about sponge cake? Sure, it doesn't taste like much and would probably be fresher and sweeter with some strawberries and cream, but at the same time it is fluffy, light, soft and moist. Wouldn't it be possible to simply enhance *these* qualities, and instead of trying to make it something it is not, try to bake the fluffiest, most wonderfully moist cake ever?

This exact way of thinking, I would say, is the reason why Japan is the world's best food destination. They not only have

their own amazing food culture, but a better version of the rest of the world's food as well. They import food ideas from China, Korea, Ethiopia, Nepal and Belgium. They refine and maximize flavor, and the result is the exact same dish, just completely different – and better. Again I see Zen Buddhism at work. Instead of being preoccupied with how something *should* be, the Japanese appreciate things for what they really are. And this doesn't just apply to food. Almost everything from jeans and Indian jewellery to mechanical watches and old motorcycles are treated this way. No one is better at appropriating other cultures than the Japanese. They are geniuses at it.

And that's how we get to the tonkatsu.

Because tonkatsu is nothing more than the Weiner schnitzel, seen through this kind of filter. It takes everything that is good about a schnitzel but raises it a notch. Instead of a thin, pounded piece of average pork, they use a thicker piece of high-quality pork, which is often of the black pig breed Kagoshima kurobuta – the wagyu of pork.

This piece of meat is then tenderized by poking thousands of holes in it – a bit like the Chinese do with their crispy pork belly. The pork is then dipped in flour, then in bright-orange egg yolk – don't get me started on the perfect Japanese eggs – then pressed down hard in panko, which is, of course, a Japanese ultra crisp version of

Tonki (p. 84)

the breadcrumb. A schnitzel *shokunin* then starts what is the real art: the deep-frying.

In Sweden, deep-fryer chefs are the nuts and bolts of the restaurant world. At a tonkatsu restaurant, he is the virtuoso. With the help of experience, presence and instinct he knows exactly when to flip, spin and take out; ten seconds longer and the piece of meat is dry; ten seconds less and you get a stomach ache.

It is precisely this expert use of the deep-fryer that strikes you the first time you eat a really good tonkatsu: how perfectly juicy the often rather lean meat really is, how much juice runs out of the meat when you dip it in a little mustard or tonkatsu sauce. After a while you also notice the sides: a bowl of steamed short-grain rice, some Japanese pickles, miso soup and a large pile of super finely cut cabbage salad with sesame dressing. This way of eating a fixed menu is called *teishoku* in Japan and is based on the traditional meals consisting of rice, soup and pickles, which are served at Zen temples.

And yes, for me, it really is like going to church.

Tonki

If you read the introduction to the tonkatsu chapter, you should know by now the dish should be served juicy. Unfortunately, I now have to confuse you because one of Tokyo's most famous tonkatsu is actually quite dry. At classic Tonki in Meguro, they have a schnitzel that is darker, more crunchy, less oily. Closer to the original tonkatsu, you could say.

Tonki originates from the golden age of tonkatsu. Tonkatsu itself has existed in Japan since the late 1800s when the Meiji administration opened up to the west and relinquished the ban on eating meat that had existed in Japan since the Middle Ages. A bunch of so-called *yoshokus* (restaurants serving Japanified western-style food) opened up all over the country. One of their dishes, tonkatsu, gained popularity and soon many traditional Japanese pubs also started serving it. Even today, tonkatsu is served at both curry and soba places, in *donburis* and pre-packaged in convenience

stores. When the Great Depression hit Japan in the '30s, tonkatsu went from being just a dish amongst others to becoming an icon – because it was the tastiest luxury item that most working families could still afford to indulge in on pay day.

That Tonki is basically unchanged since 1939 polarizes tonkatsu-Tokyo: there are those who think the place is an overrated anachronism and those who love its crunchy old-school tonkatsu. But what you lose in juiciness you win in charm. In a large, light-filled room behind a huge counter, there are around ten guys in paper hats. It is almost completely quiet, besides the sizzling of the deep-fryer and the greetings when someone new comes in. In many ways it resembles a true old American diner.

To sit and watch the routine of the deep-frying chefs is like admiring the clockwork of a Swiss watch. It just ticks. As soon as you enter, you are asked if you want *rosu* or *hire*: *rosu* (pork loin) is fattier, while *hire* (pork tenderloin) is leaner. If you have

serious heart disease, it goes without saying, you should choose the *hire*.

If there's no room at the long counter, you will be assigned a seat on one of the chairs along the wall. As soon as a seat becomes vacant, the next person in line gets to sit down in the long row of chairs. But don't get stressed out by the lack of a formal system. No one will skip ahead and no one will forget you. The staff always has everything under control. When it is your turn, the staff member points to a place, you sit down, order a biru, eat, enjoy, pay and leave.

Like most other tonkatsu places, you will get more rice, soup or cabbage if you ask, but no dessert, no coffee, no sitting around and talking for ages.

- Open every day except Tuesday 4–10.45pm
- Meguro
- 1-1-2 Shimomeguro

Taihou

Across the street from **Tonki** (p. 84) on Megurodori is Taihou, which certainly doesn't have the same iconic status as the other tonkatsu places in this book but nevertheless is a personal favorite. It is a place that more and more people are talking about. As a consequence, the queues have become longer and longer every time I walk past.

Taihou, which seen from the outside is very similar to the other places on the run-down but wonderful foodie street Megurodori, isn't particularly large, fancy or remarkable. The tonkatsu, however, is perfect, carefully made and fished out at the exact moment where it balances between too dry and too raw. The result is pork so juicy that small pools form in the cuts on the surface. Along with the crispy crust and the traditional sides, it becomes, well, sublime. Unlike the more old-fashioned tonkatsu places, Taihou also has a larger menu, including deep-fried shrimp and a rather amazing *kushi katsu* – rolled tonkatsu and leek on skewers.

- Open every day except Thursday 11.30am–2.30pm and 5.30–10pm
- Meguro
- 1-1-2 Shimomeguro

Butagumi

Butagumi has received such extensive coverage in guidebooks that it is easy to believe it's a cheap tourist trap. But nothing could be further from the truth. Instead, this beautifully faded tonkatsu pub is located in a quiet residential area that is reached by a sufficiently boring walk to keep the crowds away. Yes, if you show up for lunch, you may not even have to line up. In the beautiful wooden dining room, which is reached by a creaking staircase, you eat perfectly fried tonkatsu, beautifully served with the usual *teishoku* (set menu) sides: rice, soup, cabbage salad. As in most other places, you can choose between *rosu* and *hire*.

What distinguishes Butagumi is that instead of having pork from just one breed of pig, it has pork from as many as 50 different breeds. From domestic rare breeds such as the Kagoshima prefecture's kurobuta to Hungarian mangalitsa pig and Spanish iberico.

For those who can't get to the original, there is also a branch in fashionable Roppongi Hills. Although it's not quite as charming.

- Open every day 11.30am–2pm and 6–10pm
- Minato
- 2-24-9 Nishiazabu

Butagumi

Tonkatsu Suzuki

In Sweden, it is mostly drycleaners and cellphone-unlocking stores that are found in the subway. Eating there isn't something you like to do and for Michelin-star chef Björn Frantzén to open his new place in, say, the City Hall metro station is an absurd thought. In Tokyo, however, some of the city's fanciest places are down in the subway. The most famous example is three-star **Sukiyabashi Jiro**, known from the documentary *Jiro Dreams of Sushi*.

The biggest collection of really good, but a little more standard, restaurants can be found on Tokyo Station's Kitchen Street, which is reached by going up to level one and then walking towards Yaesu North exit. In a huge labyrinth of izakayas and sushi, noodle and tempura places, you will also find Ramen Street – an area where eight of the city's best ramen restaurants were invited to open branches – and Tonkatsu Suzuki.

Tonkatsu Suzuki is neither exclusive nor especially old-school charming. But they have one of the city's best tonkatsu dishes, an immensely scrumptious home-cooked Worcestershire-like tonkatsu sauce and two kinds of dressing for the finely shredded cabbage (the sesame dressing is best). And precisely because it is located in the travel hub Tokyo Station with its 28 platforms, most travelers will pass through here at some point during their stay. It is especially perfect on the way to or from the airport: the queues are well-oiled and fast, there is a special space for suitcases, and if you're in a rush you can take away the tonkatsu as *ekiben* (bento box).

- **o** Open every day 11am–11pm
- **d** Chiyoda
- **a** 1F Kitchen Street, Tokyo Station

寿司

SUSHI

The icon of Japanese food culture

Sushi is the icon of Japanese food culture and for many people it's the only Japanese dish they know. Therefore, it is ironic that it is also the most difficult thing to give tips about in Tokyo. Of course, cheap sushi can be found in every convenience store, and there are over 5,000 average sushi restaurants in Tokyo, compared to 500 McDonald's locations.

But if you want to eat the kind of high-quality *omakase* sushi with Michelin stars that every Tokyo traveler puts high on their to-do list, it requires more than just knowing the name of a good restaurant. Booking a table at a really good sushi restaurant requires patience, anticipation and personal relationships – alternatively a fat wallet, shiny credit card or expensive hotel concierge.

Booking a table at one of the handful of the absolute best, most modern sushi places is so difficult that you either must have been there before, know someone who knows someone who's been there before or be a member of the Yakuza. Sushi at that level is not as much dinner as a lifestyle, like sailing, collecting art or golf. It requires knowledge, dedication and interest, and for that exact reason it is difficult to write about it in a guidebook. If you still want to book a table at a high-class sushi restaurant during your Tokyo trip, I have talked to sushi chef Carl Ishizaki about the best way to approach this (p. 96).

Of course, all this doesn't mean that sushi isn't good. It is. Really good sushi can even be the best thing in the world. But if you don't have a special interest, maybe you should skip the swankiest places and instead ask your concierge about somewhere that offers a nice experience? In the beginning sushi was a simple street food; even today you could say that the more old-fashioned a place is, the larger the sushi pieces.

The selection of fish is so much larger in Japan, the craft more precise and they have both more variety and more seasons – they're said to work with 36 seasons. This means that the quality of fish and seafood is so incredibly high in Tokyo that every divey izakaya serves better fish than most of what you can find in Europe.

Nemuro Hanamaru

Chirashi *sushi at Sushi no Midori*

Nemuro Hanamaru

Conveyor-belt sushi, *kaiten-zushi* in Japanese, is popular amongst tourists because you avoid the hassle of incomprehensible menus and communication difficulties with staff. However, only real rookies pick sushi directly from the conveyer belt. If you want freshly made stuff, it is better to order directly from the sushi chef. With the exception of sushi from 7-Eleven stores, conveyor-belt sushi is often considered to be the lowest type of sushi in Japan. Hanamaru is, however, known for their quality and their purchasers have special access to much of the best fish at Toyosu Market. There are three Hanamaru restaurants in Tokyo, of which the absolute best is located in the fashionable shopping mall Tokyo Plaza. It's not possible to book a table, and it's really cheap for the quality you get – between US$1 and US$5 per piece – so expect to line up for a while.

- **o** Open every day 11am–11pm
- **d** Ginza
- **a** Tokyo Plaza Ginza 10F 5-2-1 Ginza

Sushi no Midori

One step above conveyor-belt sushi you find the slightly higher quality chain sushi. These restaurants are often large, popular places that many Japanese go to eat at. Of these chains Sushi no Midori is known as one of the absolute best value-for-money options – for a couple of ten dollar notes you get a huge portion of sushi where the quality of the fish really isn't that inferior to the much more expensive places. The difference lies in their use of simpler raw ingredients, their faster pace and that their sushi chefs aren't as dedicated. There are nine Sushi no Midori in Tokyo, the most famous being the one in Akasaka. Here, however, the queues are biblical. A wait of 2–3 hours is not uncommon, but the queue is inside and if you take a line docket you can go and do a bit of shopping in the area while you wait.

- **o** Open Monday to Saturday 11am–10pm, Sunday 11am–9pm
- **d** Akasaka
- **a** 2F 5-3-1 Akasaka

95

CARL ISHIZAKI'S SUSHI TIPS

The sushi chef Carl Ishizaki from Michelin-star Sushi Sho in Stockholm might be the Swede who has eaten at the most number of difficult-to-book sushi places in Japan. I asked him for some tips.

How do you actually get a table at a really good sushi place?
In Tokyo, the first thing they would like you to do is make a booking. This means that you either book through a booking site or in a hotel with a good concierge. You often have to book at least 2–3 months in advance. In practice however, those really serious places, where international foodies go, are impossible to get a table at if you do not know a regular who can help you get in the first time. Then you book the next visit before you leave. That's why they are fully booked all the time.

How do you choose a sushi place?
You have to do your research and try to keep track. The easiest way is to look for exciting restaurants at the concierge sites (or booking sites) and then ask the concierge at your hotel to try to book these; then you avoid the booking fee too.

What are the rookie mistakes when choosing a sushi place?
Honestly, it's a bit "newbie" to want to go to **Jiro**. And when someone comes and says that they have been to Jiro's son's place, I think, "Yeah alright, you couldn't even get a seat at Jiro?" Haha. It is very touristy there. And even though Jiro is good, it can also be a terrible experience. You come in and there are only tourists, no one looks you in the eyes, and then it's pedal to the metal: 22 pieces in 20 minutes, you take a card with Jiro written on it, then bye bye. There are maybe 10, 20 places I'd rather recommend.

So what should you do instead?
I think you should try to avoid the status hunt. One of the mistakes I made

the first time was that I wanted to go to all those super-difficult-to-book swanky places, and then I was terribly disappointed when I didn't get in. Or I had super terrible experiences when I ended up in the "tourist corner" instead of in front of the sous-chef. Especially the first few times, it is an equally powerful experience to eat at the hotel concierge's third or fourth choice. They can be awfully good, too.

Can it be difficult for a first-time visitor to go to a sushi place?
It definitely can. Sometimes they are very nice and sweet but half of what sitting at the counter is all about is interacting with the chef. They tell you about what fish you're eating and where it was caught and how they prepared it. So they get disturbed if you can't communicate properly. The best thing is actually to go with someone who speaks Japanese.

What else should you consider?
Etiquette rule number one is not biting into the sushi. Eat the whole piece in one bite. Some people eat them with chopsticks, others with their hands. Both are okay, but if you eat with chopsticks, don't massacre the sushi. Because the idea is that it goes in whole and falls apart in the mouth. Also: no elbows on the counter, don't ask for extra soy sauce and it's important to show that you appreciate the food. Many tourists are not very interested in eating, they mainly want to feed, but if you can sigh your pleasure in a convincing way, it is a fantastic icebreaker.

And what if you are used to always ordering half salmon, half avocado?
Then you shouldn't go to a sushi places in Tokyo, I think. Most do not even have any salmon.

How do you recognize good sushi?
Most places can manage the cutting techniques and the fish quality is always high. So for me, sushi is 80 to 90 percent about the rice. It should be a beautiful shape, and when you put it down it should be so loosely packed that it sags a bit; they say that it "dances". Then temperature, texture and taste are important. But everyone has different ideas.

Have you been to all your dream places?
No, absolutely not. The places I'd still like to get into are **Amamoto** and **Sugita** – where it used to be easier to get a table but they moved to a new location and upped their game. However, it is basically impossible for an ordinary tourist to book at these places. But don't forget that I am a sushi nerd and actually work with sushi.

CARL'S TOP THREE SUSHI PLACES THAT YOUR CONCIERGE SHOULD ACTUALLY BE ABLE TO BOOK:

Umi, *3-2-8 Minami-Aoyama*
"Great two-star place that wasn't super difficult to book last time I was there."

Sushi Sho Saito, *4-2-2 Akasaka*
"In short, a fantastic place. However, not to be confused with three-star **Sushi Saito**."

Sushi Nakamura, *7-17-16 Roppongi*
"Really loud but nice high-end place in tourist-packed Roppongi."

IZAKAYA

A temple devoted to the art of grazing

Many westeners have this idea that Japanese food culture is very formal, complicated, sophisticated. More recently, this idea has probably been further strengthened by all the western fine-dining restaurants that are inspired by a very Japanese attention to detail and raw materials, and also by films such as *Jiro Dreams of Sushi*. But of course it doesn't have to be like that. The fact is most Japanese restaurant visits are not at *kaiseki* restaurants and sushi places with Michelin stars, but at simple, fun, cheap neighborhood pubs where you can have a beer, eat something good and just be yourself for a little while.

An izakaya is exactly such a place. The word itself comes from "*i*" (stay/stop) and "*sakaya*" (liquor shop) – and from the beginning they were just that, small sake

stores that over time also started serving snacks with the drinks. They are often located around metro stations or in large restaurant areas – so-called *yokochos* – and are recognized by the red lanterns hanging outside, with the text 居酒屋. However, if it is 立飲み屋 on the lantern, it is a *tachinomi*, which is an extra small standing-only izakaya. Izakayas can otherwise be anything from lovely small shacks to larger traditional places where you take off your shoes and sit on tatami mats. They are always deeply rooted in everyday life, a gathering point for people in the neighborhood and an opportunity to unwind after work. A traditional British pub is perhaps the closest comparison, at least if they had served sashimi instead of Walkers salt and vinegar potato chips.

An izakaya rarely has English menus or staff who speak languages other than Japanese, and westerners won't get into some places. Therefore, they can be a bit scary for a first-time visitor. In fact, even Japanese people can feel shy about going to an unknown izakaya sometimes. But don't worry, if you don't get in to one super cozy izakaya, you just have to shrug your shoulders and go to the next super cozy izakaya, which is usually right next door.

As always, it's important to be pleasant and attentive, and not be loud, obnoxious and entitled. Instead, first poke your head through the *noren* (those curtains

in the doorway), check with the staff and hold up as many fingers as there are people in your group. When you're shown to your seat, it is usual to start with an ice-cold *nama biru* (draft beer). Add a *kudasai* (thank you) if you want to be polite. Before the beer arrives you usually get a warm towel and some kind of *otoshi* – a small snack that is added to the bill and actually works as an entrance fee, so don't get all suspicious and start complaining in a high, wronged voice. Now, it's time to order.

Although the food at an izakaya changes from place to place, the menu almost always consists of different snacks to share. Start with a couple of different things, follow your cravings and order more as you please. The usual setup is to start with pickles and other vegetable dishes, switch to raw fish and grilled meat and finish with noodles or rice.

If they only have a Japanese menu or, even worse, the walls are full of so-called *fuda* (white or yellow signs with today's specials on them), you quite simply have to dig into the phrasebook below or hope that someone nearby speaks English and can help. Izakayas are, as mentioned, nice, loud places where everyone is equally drunk, so it is completely okay to talk to table neighbors, giggle loudly and make mistakes when you order.

A SMALL IZAKAYA PHRASEBOOK

Nama biru kudasai. A draft beer, please.
Tsukemono. Japanese pickles.
Sashimi moriawase. Mixed sashimi.
Osusume wa nan desuka? What do you recommend?
Kore kudasai. I want this, please.
Oishii! Delicious!/Tasty!/Yummy!
Okaikei onegaishimasu. The check, please.

Tatemichiya aka Punk Rock Izakaya

Everyone who has seen a music tour documentary from Japan knows how incredibly good Japanese are at rocking moderately. Japanese rock fans certainly have tight jeans and leather clothing like everyone else, but they clap politely, dance in sync and stick to their designated spot – even in a mosh pit it feels like people respect each other's space. The little izakaya Tatemichiya, between Ebisu and Nakameguro, is an example of this kind of polite anarchism. The place is called Punk Rock Izakaya because of owner Yoshiyuki Okada's love of classic punk rock, and from the speakers flow a lot of the good stuff, everything from The Clash to Teengenerate – but with the volume button at 4 rather than 11.

On the whole, Tatemichiya feels like a home-staged version of iconic NY music venue CBGB. The walls are filled with

graffiti and tour posters – but the posters are of Ramones and the filmmaker Sogo Ishii's underground films, and they are decoratively framed, and the graffiti was done by the artist and regular customer Yoshitomo Nara. The toilet is small, shabby and could have come from a seedy club at St Marks Place in New York, but the hand towels are neatly folded in a beautiful bamboo basket and the steam diffuser spreads a wonderful scent of, what is it ... sandalwood?

Yoshiyuki herself has a bleached Lars Frederiksen mohawk but is an impeccable host who ensures that your highball, sake or icy-cold beer is constantly topped up. Don't miss all the fun *shochu* drinks with flavors of everything from *shiso* to chestnut.

The food is simple but good, and since this is an izakaya, the menu consists of small dishes that you order as you want them. Here you graze on stuff like raw vegetables with miso dip, *karaage*

(fried chicken), noodles, Japanese pickles or various yakitori skewers – grilled over charcoal and not gas, of course. Tatemichiya's famous avocado steak is a vegetarian snack for the meat lover, and whatever you do don't forget to order some dried fish, which you grill yourself at a tiny table grill and dip in kewpie mayo – it tastes like an MSG factory exploded in your mouth. In short: highballs, charcoal-grilled yakitori and Japanese punk band Shonen Knife at conversation-friendly volume ... this could well be the perfect bar.

- Open every day 6pm to late, smoking allowed, English menu, reservation probably not necessary if you aren't a big group or arrive after 8pm on a weekend
- Daikanyama
- B1F, 30-8 Sarugakucho

Ginza Shimada

Tachinomis, standing-only izakayas, tend to be quite divey (but fun) places. At the tiny Ginza Shimada you can both drink *and* eat fantastic small dishes. That's because it's run by a chef who was formerly at a three-star *kaiseki* restaurant, got tired of fine-dining and instead wanted to serve really good food, at reasonable prices, to cheerfully drunk guests. At 5pm it's already packed, but there's usually a quick turnover since people are forced to stand. So don't give up.

The menu changes daily, is hand-written and is only in Japanese. But a good tip is to start by ordering *nama biru* (draft beer), sake, sashimi and soba – you should be able to say that, right? The sashimi is good and there is usually a variety on offer, while the soba is Ginza Shimada's signature dish: cold buckwheat noodles topped with a heap of grated *karasumi* (dried, salted mullet roe) – like the Italian delicacy bottarga. Then, when you've gained a bit of confidence, look at what other people are eating, point to what looks good and let the evening unfold.

- Open every day except Sunday 5–11.30pm
- Ginza
- 8-2-8 Ginza

Akaoni

Akaoni is a classic, 30-year-old izakaya that has one of the city's best sake selections. They specialize in small local producers and *namazake* – a fresh, unpasteurized kind of sake that can actually be a good starting point for inexperienced sake drinkers. Akaoni has a cute, somewhat rough old-school charm, is almost tourist free (so far) and has a tough name – Akaoni means "red devil". If you are not a sake expert or don't speak Japanese, it can be difficult to navigate the 100 sake varieties and 200 small dishes on the menu, so you could leave the choice to your waiter with an elegant, *"Osusume wa nan desuka?"* (What do you recommend?). However, if you've drunk three Asahi in your room earlier, it can be difficult to remember. In that case, try a more simple, *"Omakase"* (I'll let you decide), which isn't entirely correct unless you're at a fancy sushi restaurant but easier to remember and the staff usually understand what you mean.

- Open every day 5.30–11.30pm, it's popular so make sure you book a table
- Sangenjaya
- 2-15-3 Sangenjaya

Sanshuya

If you have no desire to drink gourmet sake or eat complicated small dishes, but just want a simple, old-fashioned, down-and-dirty izakaya where it feels like you could encounter Takeshi Kitano in the movie *Sonatine*, then head to metro stations, residential areas or, pretty much anywhere really. Go on an izakaya hunt! One of the most well known, and best, is Sanshuya in Ginza, which, despite the slightly fancy surroundings, is located in a dark alley and is full of workers and ordinary people who are having a couple beers and eating some raw fish.

Sanshuya has been around since the '60s and may not be the nicest of places, but the food is good and cheap, the beer is cold and the old Tokyo–charm is undeniable.

- Open every day except Sunday 11.30am to late
- Ginza
- 1-6-15 Ginza

Sanshuya

Sanshuya

Ginza Shimada

TOKYO'S YOKOCHOS

Literally, *yokocho* means an "alley behind a main street", but the word is also used to describe the old-fashioned pub areas that are scattered throughout the Japanese cityscape. They are found all over the country but most can be found in Tokyo: under subway tracks, in narrow alleys and in the run-down old shanty towns and black markets that were temporarily built after large parts of Tokyo were destroyed during WWII. They are a remnant of Showa-era Tokyo and a living anachronism.

But Tokyo's *yokochos* are not just old school. The dark alleys, red lanterns and neon lights reflecting in rain-wet asphalt are also the archetypal images of the chaotic futuristic Tokyo you find in science-fiction films. Everywhere else in the world you would prefer to avoid these areas. But in Tokyo, they are some of the nicest, most cheerful and most relaxed places you can hang out. This is where you go for a couple of unpretentious beers after work, where you sit on beer crates, loosen your tie and talk shit with staff and strangers.

Traditionally, *yokochos* have mainly been places for an older crowd but in recent years they have begun attracting younger people, places like **Ebisu Yokocho** (p. 107) and **Niku Yokocho** (p. 45) are great examples.

Ebisu Yokocho

Ebisu Yokocho isn't literally in an alley but an old '70s shopping center
that has been converted into a modern *yokocho* with a retro style aimed
at a slightly younger and cooler crowd. Here, there are 21 loud pubs and
izakayas focusing on everything from *okonomiyaki* and grilled *gyutan* (beef
tongue) to an incredible vegetarian natural-wine bar. Ebisu Yokocho is a good
first-time *yokocho*.

- Open most days, usually from 5pm to late
- Ebisu
- 1-7-4 Ebisu

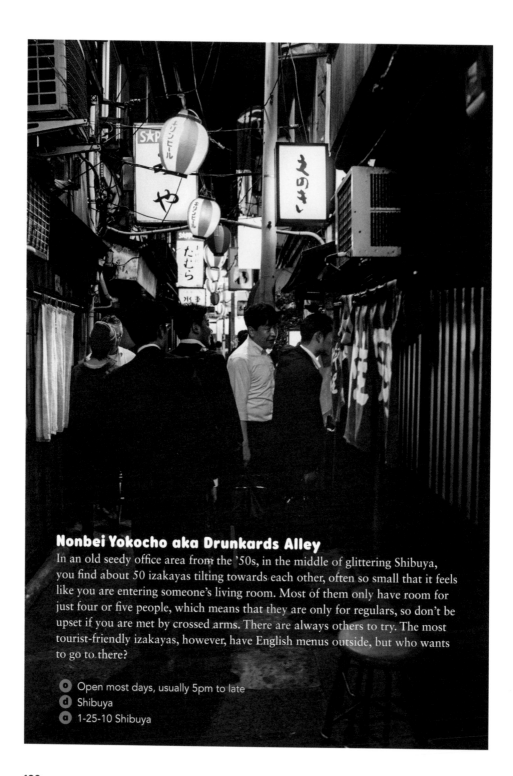

Nonbei Yokocho aka Drunkards Alley

In an old seedy office area from the '50s, in the middle of glittering Shibuya, you find about 50 izakayas tilting towards each other, often so small that it feels like you are entering someone's living room. Most of them only have room for just four or five people, which means that they are only for regulars, so don't be upset if you are met by crossed arms. There are always others to try. The most tourist-friendly izakayas, however, have English menus outside, but who wants to go to there?

- ⓞ Open most days, usually 5pm to late
- ⓓ Shibuya
- ⓐ 1-25-10 Shibuya

Yurakucho Gado-shita

A *yokocho* located under the metro tracks is called *gado-shita*, "under the beams". One of the most famous *gado-shita* lies between Shinbashi and Yurakucho metro stations near Ginza. This is truly heaven for Tokyo's office workers. The food is not particularly good, but the beer is cold and cheap and the atmosphere great – in some aspects it's a pure *Blade Runner* atmosphere. In addition to a lot of izakayas, there are also drinks vending machines outside and enormous karaoke skyscrapers.

- **ⓘ** Varies, some places are open 24 hours
- **ⓓ** Shinbashi
- **ⓐ** Between Shinbashi and Yurakucho metro stations

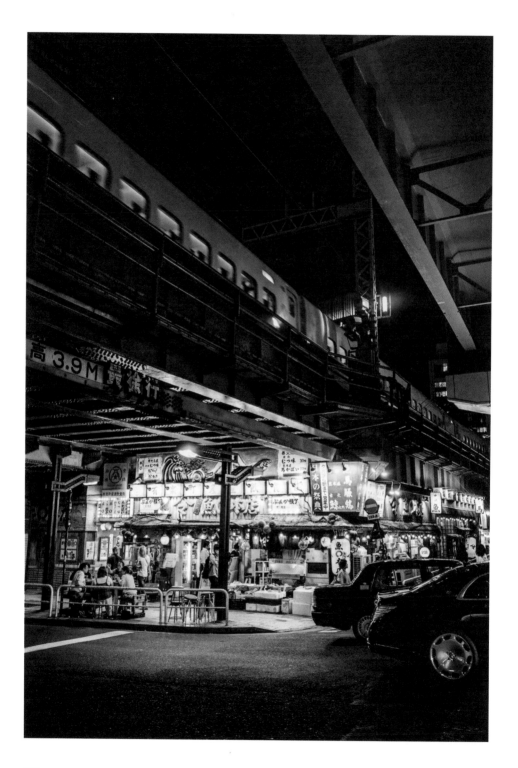

FAST FOOD & SWEET TREATS

Re-imagined goodies

Much of Japanese fast food originates in a style of cooking called *yoshoku*. *Yoshoku* literally means western food, and consists of a variety of dishes that are all adapted to Japanese taste. Some are hardly thought of as foreign anymore, such as *tonkatsu* or tempura, while others are obvious culinary crossbreeds, such as rice with ketchup or "*hambagaa*" – an early *yoshoku* version of the hamburger.

As so many other things in Japanese food culture, *yoshoku* emerged during the Meiji restoration. When Japan resumed trading with other countries and established contact with the US, the Japanese were shocked at how much taller and larger than them Americans were. The US diet was thought to be the cause, and the emperor immediately gave the order to change to a more western food approach. This attitude survived until the '70s when McDonald's

first opened in Japan with the argument that their burgers would make the Japanese as tall as the Americans. It was said that after eating hamburgers for a thousand years the Japanese would even have blond hair. In neighboring countries like China and Korea, they weren't as open to western influences, which had the consequence that these countries' food cultures are still mostly unaffected. In Japan, on the other hand, they have become world champions at taking things from other countries, changing them a little and then creating something that is still exactly the same but completely different.

This also applies to their sweets. Virtually all Japanese pastries have western origin, even if they come in wonderfully fluffy, re-imagined versions. The original candy in Japan is called *wagashi*, which literally means "fruit and nuts" but has come to mean traditional snacks of mainly three types: sweet rice cakes, hard sugar candy and gelatin desserts. Today it takes 12 years to become a *wagashi* chef and the small works of art are mainly eaten with tea and at tea ceremonies. If you want to buy *wagashi*, or any Japanese food really, go to the department store Isetan in Shinjuku and wander through its huge food market in the basement.

Henry's Burger

Henry's Burger is the chef Kentaro Nakahara's tiny hamburger place right across the street from the clothing store Evisu in Daikanyama. Only four seats and two types of burger – a single and a double, both made with A5 wagyu of the same quality as their main restaurant **Sumibi Yakiniku Nakahara** (p. 38). The meat is coarsely ground and fried like at Smashburger, which is unusual in Tokyo's hamburger circles, but fits nicely with the fatty, flavorful meat and gives a wonderfully crispy, salty crust. The rest of the burger is just simple American-style: fluffy bun, cheese, tomato, salad and dressing. For around US$9 you get a burger, fries and soft drink. For US$2 extra you get a double.

- Open every day except Tuesday
  11am–8pm
- Daikanyama
- 1-36-6 Ebisu-Nishi

Delifucious

"Burger by a sushi chef" is the motto of this fast food place in Nakameguro. The founder Shinya Kudo is a former sushi chef from two-star **Harutaka** in Ginza, and he still travels to the market every morning to get fresh fish for his tasty fish burgers. He also uses classic sushi techniques, like for his *konbujime* fish burger, where he marinates the fish in rehydrated *konbu* (seaweed) for extra taste and umami before deep-frying or roasting them "*saikyo-yaki*" style (with miso) and stuffing them in amazingly fluffy bread with coleslaw and a secret tofu sauce. His so-called *anago* dog is also worth mentioning: a tempura-fried piece of eel in a hotdog bun with julienned cucumbers or traditional *unagi* sauce.

- Open every day except Wednesday
  12–9pm
- Nakameguro
- 1-9-13 Higashiyama

Wagyu Mafia the Cutlet Sandwich

Wagyu Mafia is a members-only restaurant that is perhaps best known for having bought the most expensive Kobe cow in the history of food for its members. Now they have started a standing-only fast food place open to everyone, where they only serve the restaurant's signature dish: wagyu *katsu sando* – wagyu sandwich. Depending on the details, they cost between US$45 and US$165 and are served with Alba truffle fries.

o Open every day except Tuesday 11am–9pm
d Nakameguro
a 1-26-1 Kamimeguro

CHAINS & STREET FOOD

Ending up at a chain restaurant is usually a huge defeat for the food-loving traveler. But that is not true in Tokyo. Here it is actually quite fun to eat at fast food chains. Even American hamburger places have food that sounds appetizing. The fries are, for example, seasoned with good stuff such as chicken consomme or melted butter and soy sauce, and Japanese Burger King sells a completely black burger, Wendy's has a foie gras burger and McDonald's has a hefty shrimp burger called ebi filet-o. The domestic chain Mos

Burger even serves a burger with rice instead of bread and yakiniku instead of a meat patty. Japan's equivalent to burgers, if there is such a thing, is a *gyudon*, which is a rice bowl with meat and onions, topped with good stuff like poached eggs, *beni shoga* (pickled ginger) and spring onion. Unbelievably good to gobble up after an evening on the town and perhaps the fast food dish (after *onigiri*) that I'd most prefer to see imported to Sweden. Here are some of my other favorites.

Ichiran's *tonkotsu* ramen is so popular that there are currently 65 locations in Japan and several in the US, Europe and the rest of Asia.

Gyudon is a real fast food favorite. Look for chains like **Sukiya**, **Matsuya** or **Yoshinoya** – the latter was founded in 1899!

Chuka is the re-imagined Japanese version of Chinese food and there are simple, small, good joints on every street corner. The *dandan* noodles are a favorite.

Crazy Instagram-optimized fast food, such as a wobbly stack of pancakes, rainbow crepes or half-meter fries, can be found in and around Harajuku.

HOW TO MAKE GYUDON AT HOME

Gyudon is addictive. Apparently, all it takes is one visit to **Sukiya** or **Yoshinoya** in Tokyo, and you'll have dreams about the divine rice bowl when you get home. The good news is that it is possible to make at least as good *gyudon* at home.

Dashi is a Japanese broth that can be bought in powder form, and you can find mirin and rice wine vinegar at your local Asian grocer. The soy sauce must be a light Japanese soy sauce; if you use Chinese mushroom soy sauce it tastes awful.

INGREDIENTS, SERVES 4

5 fl oz (150 ml) Japanese soy sauce
5 fl oz (150 ml) mirin
5 fl oz (150 ml) dashi, from powder
1 tablespoon rice wine vinegar
1 garlic clove, sliced
1 inch (2½ cm) piece ginger, sliced
cooking oil for frying
1 brown onion, cut into thin segments
10 oz (300 g) entrecote or sirloin steak,
  cut into paper-thin slices
freshly cooked short-grain rice
  (sometimes sold as sushi rice)
4 egg yolks
1 leek, julienned (finely sliced and
  preferably refreshed in ice water)
beni shoga, red pickled ginger
  (sold at Asian grocers)

1. Start by cooking a *tare* (sauce) by simmering the soy sauce, mirin, *dashi*, vinegar, garlic and ginger for about 20 minutes. Strain.

2. Heat the oil in a deep frying pan. Lightly fry the onion. Then add the thinly cut meat and let it brown a little. Pour the *tare* over the meat and let it cook for a couple of minutes.

3. Serve by placing the freshly cooked rice in a bowl. Add the meat and just the right amount of *tare*, and top with 1 raw egg yolk, leek and lots of bright-red *beni shoga*.

Savoy

The world's best Neapolitan pizza doesn't come from Naples but from the small Japanese eight-seat pizza place Savoy, five minutes' walk from tourist-packed Roppongi. In addition to a selection of antipasti, there are only two pizzas on the menu: Margherita and marinara. And in normal cases I would never recommend that anyone choose pizza without cheese, but Savoy's marinara is so minimalistic, brilliant and mind-blowingly good that I have to make an exception. Succeeding in making a pizza with just tomato sauce, oregano and garlic into one of the world's best, shows just how mindful the Japanese are when they cook.

- **o** Open every day 11.30am–3pm and 6–10.30pm
- **d** Azabu-Juban
- **a** 3-10-1 Motoazabu

Himitsudo

Kakigori consists of super thin, shaved ice, flavored with different purees, juices, powders and dairy products. Incredibly good. At Himitsudo, in the super cosy area of Yanaka Ginza (don't miss the Asakura Museum of Sculpture nearby), they take *kakigori* more seriously than most. The ice comes from the city Nikko and is shaved into a light snow by two manual antique machines. There are always 132 different handmade toppings that change with the season, for example green tea and cherry blossom, purple sweet potatoes and caramel or raspberry and yogurt. The classic, however, is their *ichigomilk*, strawberries and milk, for about US$8.

ⓘ In summer open every day except Monday 11am–8pm; in winter open every day except Monday and Tuesday 11am–6pm
ⓓ Yanaka Ginza
ⓐ 3-11-18 Yanaka

Centre the Bakery

Do you also secretly love sandwich bread and eat it only when Sébastien Boudet isn't looking? If so, a visit to Center the Bakery is recommended, a temple dedicated to everything that is square, tasteless and without nutritional value. Here you can eat sublime Japanese egg sandwich, club sandwich and croque madame. They also have an incredibly good cream and fruit sandwich (see picture) and a toasted bread *omakase* with four kinds of butter, your own toaster and a glass of milk. The crusts are served on the side, of course. Sandwich bread, or *shokupan* as it is called in Japan, is another thing that the Japanese have elevated, and as proof of it, the winding queue is always long. Sandwich-bread lovers of the world, unite and take over.

- Open every day 10am–7pm
- Ginza
- 1F, 1-2-1 Ginza

Dominique Ansel Bakery

Bakers who are obsessed with sourdough and small-scale, stone-ground heritage spelt wheat won't get much out of Tokyo (yet). New York baker Dominique Ansel is a better fit for this city – a man who has given the world the cronut and whose imaginative Willy Wonka–baking lies somewhere between wacky Harajuku and fashionable Omotesando. Here, the egg sandwich is perfectly wobbly, the tomato bread looks just like a tomato and you drink your milk from an edible chocolate-cake cup – which, as an added bonus, is extremely good. Everything at Dominique Ansel Bakery is more or less Instagram optimized, and the bakery's s'mores-burner boy (see picture) is probably one of Tokyo's most Instagrammed restaurant workers.

- Open every day 10am–7pm
- Omotesando
- 5-7-14 Jingumae

THE GOURMET'S GUIDE TO THE CONVENIENCE STORE

Even if there hadn't been so much other good food in Tokyo, I would be completely satisfied with living on what I can find in the local convenience store. In Sweden, I wouldn't even want to buy an apple at 7-Eleven, but in Tokyo I even happily eat sushi from there.

Eating convenience store sushi may sound like an exaggeration, but in Tokyo it is actually a thing. There are sushi connoisseurs who know when and where the absolute best, most valuable sushi is laid out on the shelves, and then it can be become an outright stampede.

And sushi is far from the only thing that is good at convenience stores in Tokyo. *Onigiris*, the rice balls with filling, for example, are better at the convenience store than at *onigiri* places, due to an ingenious packaging that keeps the nori sheet crispy. The deep-fried stuff is shockingly crispy; the steamed food, surprisingly soft; and the beer, admirably cold. I have a long list of things I always have to eat from the convenience store and here are my 10 favorites.

An *onigiri* and an iced tea is not only an extremely good snack, it is also a perfect umami packaged-food pairing on par with sushi and sake.

Japanese convenience store egg sandwiches are egg sandwiches taken to the highest level. So fluffy, buttery and eggy that it defies description.

Japanese pickles are a favorite. Always buy a bunch to nibble on with a cold beer before you go out. And don't forget the soy sauce–pickled eggs!

Nikuman is the Japanese version of the Chinese *baozin*. So soft, it feels like eating away your dreams about getting a six-pack before summer.

There is no shame in eating deep-fried food at convenience stores. *Karaage* is fried chicken, and *korokke* is a Japanese version of western croquettes. Both delicious.

Eating snacks in Japan is fun! The favorite is called *senbei* and is super crispy rice crackers that are totally addictive. Look for the curry flavor ones.

Doroyakis are small Japanese versions of American pancakes but made smarter because they sit on top of each other with filling in between. My favorite is the one with butter cream and syrup, although the Japanese prefer bean filling, which I have difficulties learning to like. And no, your eyes are not playing tricks on you, Japanese donuts are dipped in sesame seeds. God bless them.

Baumkuchen sounds completely obscure but is awesome – it is an originally German sponge cake baked in thin layers around a spit that the Japanese have now made their own.

Purin, Japanese for pudding, are small delicious milk puddings that compare to crème brûlée in the same way that an average person compares to Beyoncé.

COFFEE & TEA

Drip coffee, tea ceremonies and kissaten cafes

*Little Nap
Coffee Stand
(p. 133)*

In Tokyo, you are never far from a small, cozy plywood-furnished coffee place where neighborhood baristas roast their own Ethiopian single-origin coffee.

Although most of these places are centered around an espresso machine nowadays, it is perhaps the so-called manual brewing – pour-over or drip method – that is most associated with Japanese coffee culture. So how do you actually brew a real cup of Japanese pour-over coffee? With patience.

First, the water should be heated to just over 90 degrees Celsius (194 degrees Fahrenheit). The carefully selected, fresh coffee should be ground and weighed, the filter rinsed. Then begins a long, careful process where the water is poured, from a special long-necked jug, in circles over the coffee which then starts to froth up, while it drips into a container underneath. This process can take up to 20 minutes in total for a single cup of damn good coffee.

This lengthy process, plus the fact that lighter roasted, more fruity and sour coffee beans are used, and also that the advocates of pour-over coffee are often young and ecologically aware (read self-righteous), have, of course, caused a stir amongst many traditionalists in the west, which means that the method has often received the slightly mocking epithet "hipster coffee".

However, the manual brewing method has a slightly different origin than many believe. In the beginning of the 1900s, a German housewife named Melitta Bentz got tired of gritty coffee and drilled a lot of small holes into a tin to filter the coffee through. Over time the invention evolved into a paper coffee filter that gave a clearer, cleaner taste, and this method spread rapidly throughout the world. It didn't take long before they completely stopped brewing coffee in the west and instead switched to automatic coffee makers. They were easy to operate, but the hot plate made the coffee bitter and in poorly cleaned machines the coffee oils went rancid, and together with the stale pre-ground coffee, the classic "office" coffee emerged; it wasn't very good, but it was fast and practical.

As a consequence, for a long time the dark-roasted espresso was synonymous with quality coffee in the west, while brewing coffee was mostly something for cops, office workers and dweebs who didn't understand how fucking cool it was

Little Nap Coffee Stand (p. 133)

to walk around town with a small dog in your handbag and a marshmallow latte in a paper cup.

In Japan, by contrast, Melitta Bentz's invention developed in a slightly different direction. After the end of WWII, trade with the west resumed and soon a number of small, gloomy cafes, called *kissatens*, started to appear. These were simple, smoky places for the people in the neighborhood, but the coffee, well, it was something extraordinary. Instead of focusing on efficiency and convenience, it was precision, care and good taste that mattered. The most ambitious *kissaten* owners began to import their own beans, which they roasted themselves, and a variety of brewing techniques were developed. Siphon brewers were invented. Methods for cold brewing and both paper filters and coffee pans were developed and

Sakurai Japanese Tea Experience (p. 143)

improved. Inspired by the Zen Buddhist tea ceremony, they also began ritualizing the coffee brewing, and a perfect cup of brewed coffee was a show of patience, rhythm, movement and craftsmanship – you could almost say a moment of mindfulness in everyday life.

Throughout this period, manual brewing was almost completely forgotten in the west. But when Japanese company Hario launched its hugely popular V60 pour-over kit in 2005, tattooed American hipsters began experimenting with old Chemex brewers and imported Japanese filter holders – and suddenly the old traditional method was super hot.

Today in Tokyo, there are a handful of traditional *kissatens* left, but even at more modern coffee places the coffee-brewing methods and, perhaps above all, philosophy of *kissatens* live on. Drinking a cup of coffee in Tokyo is therefore so much more than just having a coffee break. It is a cultural experience, an insight into Japanese everyday life and a moment of mindfulness.

Bear Pond Espresso

The espresso place Bear Pond in the backpacker area Shimokitazawa is infamous, not least because of all the hysterical Yelp reviews which, indignantly explain that reviewers have, indeed, NEVER been so badly treated and that they will NEVER set foot in here again. And they are, of course, partially right. The

barista Katsu Tanaka is an uncompromising espresso craftsman who controls his little six-seat kingdom with an iron fist.

The espresso is served only till 2pm, and it is only Katsu himself who makes them, otherwise he cannot guarantee the quality. Bear Pond's legendary Angel Stain – a super-concentrated, viscous chocolate sauce–like espresso – is so complicated to make that only ten are served per day. But then, it's also about conducting yourself properly as a guest: no ditzy Instagramming, no photography at all, and this is absolutely not the place flip open your MacBook and while away an afternoon. As with a popular sushi place, it's all about a quick in and out. Westerners used to the idea that "the customer is always right" can complain on Yelp or Tripadvisor.

I, of course, love Bear Pond, both for their out-of-this-world espresso and also for their passion and uncompromising standards. If you want a friendly greeting and loveless latte, you can go to Starbucks.

- Open every day except Tuesday 11am–5.30pm
- Shimokitazawa
- 2-36-12 Kitazawa

Switch Coffee

If you are still a bit agitated after **Bear Pond** (p. 130), you can calm your nerves at this friendly little neighborhood cafe where the friendly barista Masahiro Onishi roasts his own beans and offers pour-over, espresso or ice coffee with tonic. Masahiro speaks English well and always has pots with different coffee beans to sample before you decide. You can even get a glass of natural wine here if you want – Masahiro is friends with the wine professor at the natural-wine bar **Winestand Waltz** (p. 153).

Fuglen

The small two-person bench outside the cafe is also one of the coziest places to observe everyday life in Tokyo. To sit here with the sun on your face and a coffee in your hand while you watch people going to work, runners jogging down towards the Meguro River and an auntie replanting a potted plant on the stairs outside her apartment can be the perfect start to a Tokyo stay.

- Open every day 10am–7pm
- Meguro
- 1-17-23 Meguro

Switch Coffee

Fuglen

Perhaps Tokyo's best known coffee place, at least amongst Northern Europeans, might still be the Japanese satellite of the Norwegian cafe Fuglen. Just like in Oslo, Fuglen Tokyo is a combination of modern cafe, vintage design boutique and cocktail bar that functions as a safe oasis in a big confusing city – it even happens to be in Tokyo's most western-friendly neighborhood, with many Europeans living in the area and places like **Camelback** (p. 132), **Ahiru Store** (p. 152) and the trendy magazine *Monocle*'s store just a couple of croissant throws away. For concerned authenticity snobs, however, I can assure you that the area is more romantic cosmopolitan than cheap touristy.

- Open every day from 8am to late; coffee place during the day, cocktail bar at night
- Tomigaya
- 1-16-11 Tomigaya

Camelback

Japanese cafes usually only serve sweet treats which can become frustrating when you are jet-lagged and hungry. The small takeaway place Camelback however, is an exception. Here, former sushi chef Hayato Naruse creates sandwiches with great precision. Camelback's crispy baguette with prosciutto, shiso leaf and yuzu zest is sublime sandwich art, just like the sandwich with homemade lamb, bacon, coriander and sun-dried tomatoes.

But the thing that can really leave me longing is their egg sandwich: just warm, fluffy bread with a little freshly grated wasabi and a bite of perfectly sweet and salty *tamagoyaki* omelet, made sushi-style. So simple, so good. Maybe the best egg sandwich in a city filled with amazing egg sandwiches.

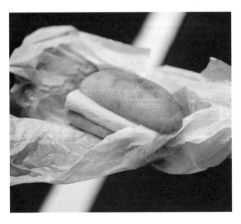

- **o** Open every day except Monday 8am–5pm
- **d** Tomigaya
- **a** 42-2 Kamiyamacho

Urara

Little Nap Coffee Stand

Idyllic Little Nap Coffee Stand is located in the middle of a relaxed residential area right by Yoyogi Park and is a dream for all of us with secret barista ambitions. Because here everything is just as you want it to be: the coffee is good, the decor is impeccable and the hang-out possibilities are endless – if Little Nap is full, just take your coffee to Yoyogi Park. Yes, even the name has that somewhat surreal English phrasing you recognize – and love – from Japanese rock band names such as Egg Murder, Spicy Socks, Swiss Porn, Gentlemen Underwear and The Almond Toe Shooters.

- **o** Open every day except Monday 9am–7pm
- **d** Yoyogi Park
- **a** 5-65-4 Yoyogi

Urara

Urara is perhaps not most known for its coffee. Instead it is probably mainly the location and the atmosphere that attracts customers. The small bohemian outdoor cafe is located in an idyllic garden in the middle of Daikanyama's shopping district and is a perfect little place to put your shopping bags under the table when you need to perk up with an espresso and a refreshing *kakigori* (flavored shaved ice) while your friends are looking for Japanese vintage fashion at Journey or indigo clothing at Okura, just a few feet away.

- **o** Open every day during summer 11.30am–8pm
- **d** Daikanyama
- **a** 20-10 Sarugakucho

Toranomon Koffee

To have a coffee here feels a bit like you accidentally got trapped in a cryo chamber and woke up in Mega City One in 2098. The cafe is located on the second floor of the hyper-modern Toranomon Hills Tower – currently Tokyo's highest point and strategically placed in the middle of an area of town that is expected to be a focus of the 2020 Olympic Games. The cafe itself consists of two minimalist wooden cubes where the coffee beans are stored in test tubes, the egg sandwiches are perfectly square, the *canelés* are futuristically cube-shaped and the baristas serve coffee dressed as space engineers on the USS *Enterprise*. Yes, sometimes it feels like at any time Will Smith can break through the roof and start chasing a robot. For coffee nerds, however, Toranomon Koffee is a sensation for other reasons, because it is the new cafe by Eiichi Kunitomo, founder of the legendary Omotesando Koffee.

Omotesando Koffee was a beautiful cube-shaped coffee bar that was built inside a traditional Japanese home in Omotesando. When it closed in December 2015, the fans literally mourned and lined up for hours in the winter cold to get one last cup of coffee. In addition to Toranomon Koffee's science-fiction qualities, the coffee is good and the place opens early, to the great delight of us jet-lagged travellers.

- **o** Open every day 7am–7pm
- **d** Toranomon
- **a** 1-1-23 Toranomon

Koffee Mameya

In **Omotesando Koffee**'s (p. 134 see **Toranomon Koffee**) old premises in the middle of Harajuku and Omotesando, Eiichi Kunitomo has now built an incredibly beautiful coffee shop: half hip coffee place, half traditional Zen garden. Here you can indeed get a cup of coffee but only to-go, and then it's either drip coffee or espresso, nothing else. Instead, the focus is on selling coffee beans. Between 15 and 20 varieties are available from the most masterful roasters from all over Japan.

The friendly staff guide you to your favorite bean by asking how you like your coffee and they get very happy if you say that you like it lightly roasted to the first crack.

The coffee beans are then placed in a beautiful little canvas bag, complete with accurate, handwritten instructions on quantity, temperature and technique. Exquisite. Now, I realize, of course, that there must be people who think it is super ridiculous to put so much effort into a cup of coffee, but then they can get stomach ulcers from acidic 7-Eleven coffee and the rest of us can have this amazing place to ourselves.

o Open every day 10am–6pm
d Omotesando
a 4-15-3 Jingumae

Café de l'Ambre (p. 138)

Café de l'Ambre

When you settle down at the curved wooden counter of this gloomy old *kissaten*, so much cool washes over you that you get dizzy: the ancient freezer that is cooled down with large ice blocks instead of electricity; the mysterious orange box that after a while turns out to be a coffee grinder; the manual scales; the well-used drip-coffee filters in flannel; the cans of coffee beans from the '70s; the bright red water jugs; the hard-set, bald man in a mustard polo shirt, gold Rolex and little finger ring that looks like a Yakuza boss in a Takashi Miike movie. Having a coffee at Café de l'Ambre is more than just a coffee break. It's an experience. The reason is, of course, the 103-year-old owner Ichiro Sekiguchi, who opened the place in 1948 after falling in love with coffee while working as a cinema operator.

From the very beginning he was a rebel and innovator. He developed techniques, questioned the norms, and if a piece of equipment didn't exist, he invented it. He has, amongst other things, rebuilt his coffee roasting machine, invented that strange orange coffee grinder and designed the long-necked coffee pot that has now become a symbol of Tokyo's *kissaten* cafes (and can be bought to take home if you want). And when a cargo of coffee beans got stuck in Siberia at the outbreak of WWII and didn't arrive in Tokyo until five years later, he thought "oh well" and tried to roast the beans anyway, and the result tasted ... excellent. Even today (or at least at the time of writing) Ichiro Sekiguchi stores and roasts his coffee beans himself, of which the oldest (at my last visit) were from 1973 – something he's perhaps quite alone in doing in an industry obsessed with freshness. Even the coffee menu reflects this kind of individuality. They only serve

coffee, nothing else, but in lots of different variations. For example, what about a coffee with a raw egg in it? Anyone? No? A plain cup of drip coffee will indeed set you back about ten bucks, but then you will also get a show in old-fashioned pour-over techniques, plus they use almost twice as many coffee beans than at the usual, modern coffee places.

- Open Monday to Saturday 12–10pm, Sunday 12–7pm
- Ginza
- 8-10-15 Ginza

Satei Hato

At the second classic *kissaten* cafe in this guidebook, it's a little less gloomy and much more cozy. At Satei Hato there's classical music coming from the speakers, odd British porcelain on the shelves, Royal Copenhagen plates on the walls and on the sofas cool old aunties sit and chain-smoke and laugh loudly. It was a visit to Satei Hato that inspired Barista James Freeman to start Blue Bottle Coffee in Oakland in the early 2000s, a coffee shop and roaster that would prove to be crucial to the craft's advancement in the world and now also has three branches in Tokyo. Of course, we all love when things come full circle! In his book *The Blue Bottle Craft of Coffee*, Freeman even writes that he "probably thinks about Satei Hato at some point every day". However, it's not just Satei Hato's atmosphere, iconic status and meticulously brewed drip coffee that makes it worth a visit – but also its cakes. Even if you normally look down on freshly baked sweets, Satei Hato's cakes are quite spectacular. And not because they have rainbow colored layers or a sculpture of Hello Kitty taking a coffee break made of fondant as decoration. But because they are so minimalistic and sublime. The Japanese are the best in the world at baking sponge cake, and Satei Hato's pound cakes, as they call them, are perfectly fluffy, wonderfully juicy and served with just a little frosting or cream.

- Open every day 11am–11.30pm
- Shibuya
- Futaba Building 1F, 1-15-19 Shibuya

Sakurai Japanese Tea Experience

Just like the way Japanese baristas are turning to the traditional *kissaten* cafes for inspiration, tea master Shinya Sakurai does a hyper-modern version of the ritual Zen Buddhist tea ceremony.

Shinya, with 14 years of traditional tea master training behind him, pairs attention to detail, ritual stirring and an incredibly beautiful *wabi-sabi* aesthetic of the tea ceremony with the modern environment and the good service of fine-dining restaurants. Here you don't have to worry about making mistakes or your legs falling asleep after sitting on your knees for 40 minutes.

Around a counter with eight seats, you can instead savor a cup of extremely high-quality Japanese sencha, matcha or gyokuro tea. Or why not try a whole tea tasting menu with snacks such as pickles and various kinds of *wagashi* (traditional Japanese sweets) for around US$40? There's even the option of drinking tea-based cocktails or a tea-based beer. And in summer

they take out an ancient *kakigori* machine, which shaves wonderfully soft, snowy ice that is flavored with roasted hojicha tea. There is also a teashop that sells beautiful ceramics and a wide range of teas from all over Japan, places where Shinya himself travels to select the products. Behind a glass wall (see below) you can also find the tea place's own tea roaster.

- **o** Open every day 11am–11pm
- **d** Omotesando
- **a** 5F Spiral, 5-6-23 Minami-Aoyama

Gen Gen An

Right in the middle of Shibuya's shopping area is Gen Gen An, a little slip-in-cafe with hip-hop on the boombox and bicycles leaning against the wall outside. At first glance, it is a completely ordinary hip Tokyo cafe, but instead of drip coffee, craft beer or limited hand-printed t-shirts featuring automatic weapons, Gen Gen An sells Japanese tea, so-called *nihoncha*. In fact, they are experts particularly in terroir-driven teas from Ureshino in the Saga prefecture, and both location and interior design are strategically planned, so people other than the usual old farts will realize how amazing Japanese tea is. And that's it. Because even though they also sell tea cocktails, stylish t-shirts and nice tea equipment, it is a quick takeout sencha I pop in for before it's time to go shopping in nearby Tokyu Hands.

- **o** Open Tuesday to Thursday 11am–11pm
- **d** Shibuya
- **a** 4-8 Udagawacho

Tokyo Saryo

Why has coffee become so big in Japan at the same time as the amazing Japanese green teas have been forgotten by the younger generation? I asked the designer Mikito Tanimoto about it, and with one foot in contemporary coffee culture and another in the traditional tea ceremony, he, together with a colleague, opened the hyper-aesthetic tea place Tokyo Saryo in the middle of the quiet residential area Sangenjaya.

Tokyo Saryo has not only become popular because they sell affordable teas and have a stylish decor, but also because they dedicate themselves to the traditional tea ceremony principles of *"wa"*, *"kei"*, *"sai"* and *"jaku"* (harmony, respect, purity and serenity). This makes a visit an almost meditative experience. They have even invented a method of brewing pour-over tea, much like you do with coffee, which is also very cool.

The menu offers only a choice of two green teas and a sweet treat for 1300 yen, which is around US$10. The teas are not only chosen by area and origin but also where the taste is on a scale of sweetness, bitterness and umami. Each tea leaf is brewed thrice, with different times and water temperatures, where the last one, at least during our last visit, was drunk with a piece of seaweed in it, which gave it almost a broth flavor and was said to be good protection against colds.

The sweets are the traditional Japanese *wagashi* kind. For lovers of loose candy, this means unexpected things like *yokan* (red bean jelly) or *ohagi* (sweet sticky-rice balls).

- Open every day 11am–8pm
- Setagaya
- 1-34-15 Kamiuma

THE JAPANESE TEA CEREMONY

It is easy to just dismiss the Japanese tea ceremony as a tourist-friendly historical remnant – a bit like railway museums and medieval fairs. But if you want to understand what makes Japanese food culture so special, it actually helps if you know the origin of the tea ceremony. In fact, even much of what we see in the west carries the DNA of the tea ceremony, from the minimalism of fine-dining restaurants with a more natural view of farming and growing food to the discerning and DIY spirit of the hipster culture. In many ways, however, it is a philosophy that is opposite to the west.

At best, in Sweden we think that people who dedicate themselves to baking with sourdough or growing potted plants have a nice hobby. At worst, they are dilettantes. According to our tradition, people are divided into those who do important things and those who mess around. Why dedicate yourself to something as pointless as brewing IPA when you can do important things like rage on the internet? Or why should you feed your sourdough when you can read an important article? This reflects our dualistic way of seeing things: you are either wrong or right, for or against, dorky or cool.

In Zen Buddhist tradition, you don't make these distinctions. You don't divide the world into "either/or". But you also don't NOT divide it into "either/or". You are, as it is called, non-dualistic. You realize that something can actually be more than one thing at the same time, and therefore don't judge what a person does, but instead try to focus on HOW they do it. And that's where the tea ceremony comes in.

At some point in the Middle Ages, the first tea plants were brought to Japan from China by – you guessed it – Buddhist monks, and they drank this new powerful drink mainly as an aid to staying awake during the long meditation sessions.

Unlike the first wandering, begging monks, these Japanese Buddhists lived in self-sufficient temple communities, where it was impossible to live a completely spiritual life because the rice field needed to be cleared, the roof had to be repaired, cooking and cleaning had to be done. So instead of disconnecting everyday life from the meditation that was central to their religion, they integrated them both.

Doing their chores simply became an extension of the sitting meditation, and they strived to be completely present, all the time. This was of course impossible, because as long as you are human your thoughts will inevitably wander. But the funny thing about meditation is that it's not about zoning out into a state of blissful calm, but instead allowing yourself to fail over and over again. Every time your thoughts stray, to bring your attention back to what is happening in exactly this moment, be that staring straight into the wall, taking a walk or brewing a cup of tea.

The Zen expression "chop wood, carry water" encapsulates this. They don't believe that spirituality is about mysterious revelations, omnipotent gods or great truths. Instead, true enlightenment is to do everyday chores like chopping wood and carrying water, but to do them sincerely, deliberately and with all your attention.

In the 16th century, a man named Sen no Rikyu was attracted to the ideas of Zen Buddhism. He was the son of a trader but rebelled against his family's materialism and began studying at a temple outside Osaka. He was impressed by how the monks found meaning and satisfaction in apparently simple things like cleaning sesame seeds or chopping firewood. But Sen no Rikyu soon chose to concentrate on one of the most routine, ordinary activities you could imagine: how to drink tea.

Tea at this time had become a luxury item and status symbol amongst the Japanese upper class. They built huge teahouses and had awfully expensive Chinese teacups made of thin, fine porcelain to impress neighbors and rivals. Sen no Rikyu questioned this kind of luxury consumption by replacing the expensive imported cups with thick, crude, irregular, handmade so-called *chawans* (matcha cups) and the palaces with simple teahouses built so small that even the most powerful people needed to bow when they entered. These teahouses were built with untreated natural materials, were located away from the main areas and were almost completely unfurnished to convey a sense of harmony and proximity to nature.

When they drank their tea, they stirred the tea according to a specific pattern to show respect for each other's personal space, and said pleasant courtesy phrases to emphasize the importance of not appearing to be someone who is more important than others. Yes, every aspect of the tea ceremony, from attentively boiling water to the ritualized measuring of the tea, reflected the Zen Buddhist teachings that everything is transient and nothing is perfect.

Even the tools they used should reflect what Sen no Rikyu called *wabi-sabi* – where *wabi* means satisfaction with the simple and *sabi* means appreciation of the imperfect. The materials were coarse, everyday materials and showed clear signs of age and use. Instead of striving for unattainable ideals such as eternal youth, perfection and immortality, the tea ceremony was simply a melancholy reminder that there is also a kind of beauty in everything that ages, breaks and dies. Instead of throwing out a teacup that had broken, they repaired it with gold-colored glue, which turned the cracks into something beautiful. Or as the singer and Zen monk Leonard Cohen put it 500 years later: "There is a crack in everything. That's how the light gets in".

CRAFT BEER, NATURAL WINE & SAKE

The artisanal and organic way of getting drunk

Ahiru store

Drinking natural wine is still quite new in Sweden. Natural-wine importers find it difficult to get their wines into Swedish wine stores, natural-wine bars are still considered a fad and old Bordeaux geezers cannot stop complaining about how sulphite-free Gamay tastes like a hamster cage. In Japan, however, they have been drinking natural wine since the '90s. Earlier, actually, than it became a thing in France. The demand for the light, fruity wines soon became so great that in the early 2000s Japan imported 75 percent of all natural wine produced in France. Today you can find natural wine everywhere in the city, from fancy pubs' wine lists and cool bars to small natural-wine places. Even the domestic wine production, which has always produced quite close to the French

natural-wine standards, has grown and begun to be redefined.

The reason, of course, is that natural wine suits the Japanese. They appreciate simple, natural products with pure taste that are produced on a small scale and with respect for nature. Of course, it helps that Japan isn't a traditional wine-drinking country with all the attendant preconceived opinions, beliefs and status associations.

Craft beer, however, hasn't had it as easy. *Ji-biru*, local beer as it's also called, still accounts for a very small part of the beer production. The reason is said to be historical. When Japan began brewing its own beer in the early 1900s, only German beer brewers were used for expertise, which means it's always been light lagers that have dominated the market. When a penalty tax was put on beer, the brewers started skimping even more on the ingredients, and this lager became even lighter (and better if you ask me). The big breweries gained an iron grip on the market and made life difficult for small producers who had – and still have – a difficult time getting into bars, restaurants and izakayas. When you add that home brewing is still prohibited, you realize that they don't have the same grass-root movements as the US and Sweden to fetch talents from. But that

Nakano Beer Kobo

has stared to change. New breweries are popping up all the time and the explosion of craft beer that we saw ten years ago in the west is happening in Tokyo now. Every month, new craft-beer bars open up, and Japanese brewers are beginning to find their own style by using local produce such as yuzu, sake yeast, sweet potatoes and plums. Considering the style of almost all other Japanese food production, my guess is this is just the beginning.

So is there an equivalent of craft beer and natural wine for sake then? Yes and no. Sake classified as *junmai* has always been brewed pure, natural and without all the additives. Only rice, water, yeast, koji.

However, there is a younger generation who believes that Japanese sake has started to become too standardized, too pleasant and pure. As sake production is becoming more and more industrialized and uses the same standardized yeast strains and rice that has been grown using artificial fertilizers and pesticides, the sake is simply getting boring. Instead, they advocate for a sake that is more playful and creative, less bound by old rules, while the techniques are more in line with traditional methods.

In the so-called *kimoto* brewing, the rice comes from unsprayed paddy fields, they use wild yeast, large wooden vats and a personal blessing for each rice grain. Brewing so-called *doburoku*, an unpasteurized, cloudy sake with large rice grains in it, is this movement's equivalent to IPA. There are even those who question whether quality sake means hard-polished rice and instead use completely natural brown rice for an even more funky, crude sake. At the center of this movement is sake sommelier Marie Chiba and her pub **Gem By Moto** (p. 157) in Ebisu. But more about that later.

Ahiru Store

In hip Tomigaya, you'll find this stylish little wine bar, which, due to massive media coverage, has become the wine bars' equivalent to the nearby cafe **Fuglen** (p. 131). So it is already quite an obvious choice for tourists in the know, but, of course, that doesn't mean it's not good. Because it is. The sommelier Teruhiko Saito has a fun natural-wine list at great prices, while his sister Wakako bakes sourdough bread and cooks wine-friendly snacks. Most of them are typical wine-bar fare; think salads, charcuterie, homemade sausages and pâtés, but of course with a Japanese twist. For example, don't miss the avocado and octopus salad with wasabi.

The only drawback is Ahiru Store's popularity; there is only one bar plus standing room for eight people, so it can be quite difficult to squeeze your way in. So show up really early or really late.

o Open every day except Sunday 6pm–12am
d Tomigaya
a 1-19-4 Tomigaya

Ahiru Store

Winestand Waltz

This natural-wine bar is not much bigger than a wardrobe and hard to find – so, two of the basic criteria for a really good Japanese bar. In fact, it is so cramped that if the person furthest in moves then everyone else does too, a bit like a more fun version of *The Human Centipede*. The walls are decorated with Jacques Tati posters, the music is classical, the glasses and plates antique, and behind the bar is Yasuhiro Ooyama – who is also known as the Wine Professor – pouring French, Italian and Japanese natural wines that he brings out from something that looks like an old refrigerator. It is one of the best bars in the world. However, due to the size of the place, you should have an alternative plan. **Ebisu Yokocho** (p. 107), for example, is close by.

Winestand Waltz

🕐 Open Monday to Saturday 6pm–12am, however, these may vary due to a generally relaxed attitude to life

📍 Ebisu

🏠 Shimada Building 1F, 4-24-3 Ebisu

Nakano Beer Kobo

Have you also always dreamed of drinking craft beer in a treehouse? If so, I recommend a visit to Nakano Beer Kobo – a wood-furnished, homemade-brew pub with the usual minimal amount of space for a Japanese bar (read: cramped). Nakano also has a small wooden loft which you can climb up to with your beer. Although it's obviously quite dangerous if you've drunk too much, it is cozy and feels a bit like you've stolen beer from your dad and are drinking it hidden up in the top of your bunk bed. *Kobo* means factory in Japanese and refers to the tiny brewery behind a glass pane that they also managed to squeeze into the premises. If you are in the mood for a bar-crawl, Nakano Beer Kobo is part of a chain of six similar wood-furnished pubs, which are all located behind the Chuo line's metro stations. However, this is the smallest and cheapest of them. All beers and all good snacks cost 500 yen (around US$5) each. You use the same beer mug all evening, and there is a machine on the bar where you can wash it.

- **o** Open Monday to Friday 6–11pm, Sunday 3–9pm
- **d** Nakano
- **a** 5-53-4 Nakano

Hatos Bar

If there were a contemporary Japanese hipster equivalent to Harry's New York Bar in Paris, this would be it. At Hatos Bar, it's always full of American expats craving biru and BBQ. In addition to craft beer – especially microbrewed ales – Hatos serves genuine American pit BBQ. And you know what? It's really good. The baby back ribs are juicy – just the right amount of sweet and smoky – and if you order a couple of the Japanese side dishes, you don't even need to feel bad about eating American food in Tokyo. The atmosphere is laidback: with dubstep music from the speakers, mismatched '50s furniture and a stylish wooden bar. *Vice*'s YouTube channel *Munchies* made a report about Hatos a while back, so maybe now you understand what kind of place it is? Being so popular, it is also quite drop-in friendly. It is located between Nakameguro and Daikanyama, in what I think is the city's nicest and best foodie area.

- **o** Open every day except Sunday 6–9pm
- **d** Nakameguro
- **a** 1-3-5 Nakameguro

Another8

Another8 is the ultra stylish Kyoto brewpub **Before9**'s newly opened branch in Tokyo. Just like Before9, it is simple, clean and full of stylish fashionistas. It is also one of the few places in this book that is big enough to bring the whole gang to, although in that case, don't tell them you got the tip from this book. On the whole, this place feels quite tourist friendly with its English menu, simple design and light types of wood, with one exception – around where you'd normally find the coat check, that's where you buy beer, from one of eight taps. The beers change constantly, but a beer from Kyoto Brewing is always part of the mix. Drinking beer without snacks is barbaric, so Another8 also has a really good selection of small dishes and a small but good sake list.

- **o** Open every day except Tuesday 5pm–1am
- **d** Meguro
- **a** 1-2-18 Shimomeguro

Hatos Bar

Nakano Beer Kobo

Another8

Another8

Gem by Moto

If you are interested in modern, craft-driven sake, you must go to Gem by Moto. The place is run by a completely female staff led by the sake sommelier Marie Chiba, a former biochemist who became interested in sake and is now a prominent figure for a new movement trying to reinvent the tradition-bound beverage. She appears in a sake documentary and one issue of the ambitious Japanese magazine *Rice* was almost entirely devoted to her. She even has her own manga: *Nihonshu ni koishite* (in love with sake).

Marie is so passionate that when she once managed to get a table at **Sushi Kimura** – a legendary upscale and hard-to-book sushi place – she brought along 30 bottles of sake and gave the staff careful instructions on how and when they should be opened. Of course, Mr Kimura was extremely annoyed. But when the dinner started, the master was impressed by her knowledge and passion, and now they collaborate on a regular basis.

Marie is devoted to something she calls "mouth flavor modification". In Japan, they have a tradition of drinking sake while still having food in the mouth. Marie has just refined this idea and made it a policy at Gem by Moto – here, sake isn't just something you drink alongside the food; you drink it together *with* the food and sometimes it even works as a sauce. Gem by Moto's signature dish, for example, is a ham croquette with blue cheese that is eaten with a glass of *doburoku* – a cloudy, yoghurt-scented, rice-porridge-looking sake that you almost have to chew. It's pretty wonderful.

An evening here, however, requires an adventurous mind and you must be prepared to put both beverage and food choices, and your whole night really, in Marie and her colleagues' hands. But in that case, you get an amazing experience and a crash course in sake knowledge, where it's not unusual to sit next to the person who made the sake you are drinking.

- Open Tuesday to Friday 5pm–12am, Saturday and Sunday 1–9pm
- Ebisu
- 1-30-9 Ebisu

HOW TO LEARN TO LOVE SAKE

Sake is as exciting a cultural drink as wine, yet it is difficult to get some people to drink it. They think it's tasteless and stale, but to judge all sake by something you got wasted on in college is like dismissing Italian cuisine after eating canned spaghetti and meat sauce. Sake is a fantastic and exciting drink. It has wine's tradition and terroir, and craft beer's lovely DIY spirit. You can drink it ice cold to warm, crystal clear to cloudy. And even though it took a while, I am now a fully-fledged sake advocate. So here's how you can become one, too.

1. Drink it with food

So, why do you really have to learn to like something that's already a treat? It's a bit like forcing yourself to start eating M&M's and Skittles. The reason, of course, is: umami. If there is something that characterizes Japanese food, it is the umami. In fact, Japanese food is so umami-laden that after a week in Tokyo you begin to look down on all the other, weaker flavors.

Umami is quite simply the best, but it has a big disadvantage: it is difficult to match with wine. But do you know what suits umami excellently? That's right, sake. This is why I think Japanese food in Sweden is often remarkably unsatisfactory – instead of forcing people to drink sake, they adapt their food and make it more wine-friendly. Boooring! So start drinking sake when you go out to eat.

2. Drink a lot of sake

What is actually the secret behind all the great sommeliers' finely tuned tastebuds and razor-sharp ratiocination? Easy. They have drunk copious amounts of wine. Like, a bizarre amount. Really good sommeliers wouldn't have gotten to where they are if they'd never drunk Chassagne-Montrachet with their breakfast cereals.

I would be less worried if my daughter came home and said she wanted to become a navy SEAL than if she had started a WSET (Wine & Spirit Education Trust) course. Now, of course, I don't encourage anyone to devote themselves to alcohol consumption at that level. And by the way, the sommelier spits out the wine (or so they claim). But the fact is that they have a point: if you really want to get to know something you have to expose yourself to it. A lot. So when you are in Tokyo, be sure to go to places with lots of sake, and also lots of good sake. Start by trying to ignore what it is you're drinking, and instead just let the impressions and flavors wash over you.

3. Gain a "taste"

What happens when you eat or drink lots of something is that you start to notice the differences; details are crystallized and slowly but surely you begin to develop a "taste". You realize that you prefer IPA over stout beer, Burgundy over Bordeaux wine. What makes sake a little more complicated is of course the labels. If you think it is difficult to decipher the label of a syrah from Languedoc-Roussillon, try to distinguish a 純米酒 from a 大吟醸酒. People often make it a bit too advanced too fast, and start talking about classes and how much the rice is polished, *junmai* and *daiginjo*. I think it's easier to start by asking yourself what you actually like. Do I like my sake fruity or dry? Umami-packed or pure? Do I like it unpasteurized and funky or pasteurized and balanced? Beware, however, of making any assumptions – just because you like dry wine doesn't mean you like dry sake, and a natural-wine drinker may prefer more traditional sake.

JAPANESE BARS

From cocktail bars in Ginza to broom closets that sell shochu shots

Even if Tokyo didn't have yakiniku and yakitori, and even if they didn't have tonkatsu, gyoza, sushi or any of the other types of food I write about in this book, I would still come here just for the bars. With the exception of maybe Austin and New Orleans, Tokyo has the best bars in the world. And they are everywhere.

Tokyo is estimated to have 16,000 bars, most of them tiny. Sometimes Tokyo feels like a city built on bars. You walk down a staircase and there is a secret door leading to a cloakroom-sized gin bar where a

surly bartender in a dress suit is carving a perfect diamond out of ice. You take the lift up eight floors, walk along a carpeted, fully covered exterior corridor and behind an apartment door you will find an exact replica of the library in a Scottish whiskey distillery. You walk down to the recycling bins at your Airbnb apartment to throw away your bottles, and there's a chubby dude with dreadlocks playing dub reggae and selling shochu shots.

The bars aren't just everywhere, you can find all types as well. From the upscale classic cocktail bars in Ginza where bartenders in bow ties do the "Tokyo hard shake", to simple beer-and-shots bars improvised in someone's garage, to all the wonderful music bars with walls full of vinyl records specializing in psych rock, classical music or Ethiopian jazz. Then of course we have all the wacky bars: there are bars where you can cuddle cats, hedgehogs, owls and penguins. There are bars with broad themes; such as ninjas, railways or robots; and bars with specific themes such as the prison hospital at Alcatraz. There is a bar whose thing is conveyor-belt sushi – but at high speed – and there is a bar that at first seems completely normal, until you realize that the serving staff consists of trained macaques – yes, monkeys!

Going on a bar-crawl in Tokyo is simply like jumping into the rabbit hole and poking your head out in Wonderland while

simultaneously getting kicked in the nuts by the Cheshire cat.

And best of all is that, unlike that amazing country bar in Austin or the wonderfully divey speakeasy in New Orleans, you don't risk your life when you go out. Tokyo is one of the world's safest cities, and for a western man used to drunken idiots at the pub it is oddly liberating to be able to walk around without anyone wanting to fight you. But just because Tokyo is so safe doesn't mean that you should bring the kids. Not that they wouldn't have fun, they would, but because you wouldn't. Also, in Tokyo you are not allowed to bring children to bars and sometimes not even restaurants. You just accept that there are actually pleasures that are only for adults. Quite simply, Tokyo takes its bar culture seriously.

The reason, I think, is that they have such a long tradition. When Japan opened up to the west at the end of the 19th century, it coincided with the newly emerging American cocktail culture.

But when that abruptly ended in the US in the '20s with Prohibition, it continued to develop in Japan. In the west bartending is still a job for young people, but it is a career in Japan, something where you start out as an apprentice and then dedicate yourself to the craft until you are a master. Again, if you do something, you do it well; there is always clearer ice to freeze, a more perfect gin and tonic to create or a more effective, more elegant way to dry the bar.

And somewhere in Tokyo, right now someone is trying.

Little Smith

When you think of Japanese cocktail bars, you think of Little Smith. It's down in a basement in Ginza, the lights are dimmed, the drinks are classic and the bartender wears a white tuxedo jacket and bow tie and does the Tokyo hard shake – a shaking technique invented by the legendary bartender Kazuo Uyeda that is said to make your cocktail ten percent colder. Where the nearby **Bar High Five** (p. 164) is beginning to feel like a language school for bartenders, Little Smith remains old-school. Pulling open the heavy door, sitting at the elegant wooden bar and ordering an old fashioned makes you feel cool and distinguished like Ann-Margret, Frank Sinatra or, in my case, Edvard Persson.

And how elegant it is! The bartender puts as much effort into pouring a glass of water as mixing a martini, and their bloody mary made with fresh tomatoes might be the best in the world. There is only one drawback: it is expensive. And the good drinks, comfortable bar stools and the smooth service make it easy to stay until you've maxed out your Amex.

- Open Monday to Friday, 6pm–3am, Saturday 6pm–1am
- Ginza
- KN Building B2F, 6-4-12 Ginza

Chilita

This may not be a bar worth crossing the city for ... unless you are as obsessed with weird teeny-tiny bars as I am.

In Sweden, you generally can't start a profitable restaurant without being backed by a restaurant group, leasing a huge venue and having it decorated by a concept agency into an inauthentic French bistro. In Japan, it's enough that you have a passion for it. Even if you only have one room, you are free to do what you want with it, no matter how small it is. It could, for example, be used as a bicycle garage, for waste sorting or, as in the case of Chilita, to start a combined antique shop, chili-dog

stand and improvised bar, where it's mainly your friends hanging out but where it's not super awkward – well, maybe just a little – when a Swede suddenly appears. Chilita is so small that you have to sit on pallets, and the ceiling height is so low that the guy playing Holger Czukay on the laptop has to crouch. It is quite wonderful and it's located right across from the bar **Hatos** (p. 154) if you want to visit both in one night.

- Open every day 1–11pm
- Nakameguro
- 1-2-14 Nakameguro

Ben Fiddich

Inside an apartment building, up nine floors and behind a mysterious door, you step into a dark room with Renaissance paintings and a stuffed deer head on the wall, bottles with frothing concoctions on the shelves, dried mandrake hanging from the ceiling and cembalo music flowing from the speakers.

If **Little Smith** (p. 164) represents the old-school Japanese cocktail bars, Ben Fiddich represents the new. First of all, it's not in Ginza but in Shinjuku. And where the Ginza bars are dedicated to classic cocktails and techniques, the bartender Hiroyasu Kayama is just as elegant but considerably more progressive.

He makes infusions, decoctions and tinctures with seasonal vegetables, fruits and herbs, and he uses a mortar and pestle as often as a shaker when he mixes his drinks. There are no menus. Instead you get the question whether you want a drink based on whiskey, gin, absinthe or amaro. When you've answered, he gets to work: a carafe with something unidentifiable is taken down, a bottle of whiskey is opened, something that could be juju berries is muddled and suddenly the most beautiful, most adorable drink is in front of you. You are just about to take a sip when Kayama stops you. He sprinkles a tiny flake of a dried, unidentifiable herb that he lets slowly sink down into your cocktail. Now it is ready. Now it is perfect. And so it continues. With drinks that feel improvised, as if they were invented in the moment together with you.

All you have to do is sit back and listen to the lute music.

- Open every day except Sunday 6pm–3am
- Shinjuku
- Level 9, 1-13-7 Nishi-Shinjuku

Bar Gen Yamamoto

This is one of Tokyo's most talked about bars. But I would like to give a warning: there is about the same chance that it will be a transformative experience as that it will leave you with a vague feeling of the *Emperor's New Clothes*.

Or maybe you will experience it like I did: a little of both. Because the drinks here are so minimalistic, so simple and subtle that it sometimes feels like you're drinking smoothies in the home of a friend who's got a new juicer. Only to shake you to the core a second later.

Unlike an ordinary Japanese bar, there isn't an atmosphere of Prohibition here, but rather it's of a Zen garden. There is no music and, besides the counter and a small stone plate with a flower, the only interior design is Gen Yamamoto himself. He gets out fruits, bottles, glasses and tools only when he uses them, and they are put back just as fast. It is elegant and meditative, like a tea ceremony, and about as intoxicating. Because even though you can only choose between two *omakase* menus – with four or six drinks respectively – you will hardly leave here drunk.

The drinks are small. It is also not a place where you order an Orgasm on the Beach. Instead, it's constantly changing, nameless cocktails based on locally grown fruits and vegetables that are prepared simply. Sometimes an apple is grated and the juice is mixed with a Swiss craft gin. Or a mandarin is pressed and heated with shochu and small pieces of daikon. It is brilliant and underwhelming, and is more like a visit to a progressive *kappo* restaurant than a crazy night on the town.

- Open every day except Monday 3–11pm
- Azabu-Juban
- 1-6-4 Azabu-Juban

Ben Fiddich

Bar Gen Yamamoto

Track Bar and Bar Martha

Track Bar is the kind of bar that makes you wish you'd just been dumped. Not because it's a good place to pick-up, but because it's a perfect bar to mend a broken heart. It's dark, cool and subdued. The walls are covered with vinyl records which the bartenders would rather browse through than actually serve the guests. But it is okay, because then they put on "Flamenco Sketches" by Miles Davis or "The Only Living Boy in New York" by Simon & Garfunkel, and they play it on a very old hi-fi system that looks like it could belong to a 65-year-old American university professor with serious audiophile interests. Yes, here you can devour music, drink beers and shots without anyone trying to cheer you up or thinking you are strange. In fact, you'd be more likely to be cheering the place up.

Because Track Bar is one of the places that consistently gets bad Yelp reviews due to westerners' unreasonable expectations of service. People get angry because a group of drunken louts was denied entry, the bartender refused to take a selfie or they got kicked out after requesting a song by Diplo. And Track Bar is really quite strict about certain things: you are not allowed to take photos, play on your cellphone, be louder than the music or wear sandals.

But, they offer very good snacks! Nearby is **Bar Martha** – a similar place by the same owners but with even more focus on music. There are a handful of other bars in this small audiophile bar chain around Tokyo. Check out the website to see if one is close to you (www.marth-records.com).

- Open every day 7pm–5am
- Ebisu
- Track Bar, 3-24-9 Higashi; Bar Martha, 1-22-23 Ebisu

THE MOVING CASTLE

When talking about Tokyo's bar life, it is impossible not to mention Golden Gai. Now, the Golden Gai is not ONE bar but about 250 – all tightly packed into an area about the same size as a large parking lot outside a supermarket. Even if you are a teetotaller, Golden Gai is fascinating. The small, dilapidated two-story houses occupying six streets in the middle of hyper-modern Shinjuku have miraculously been spared from earthquakes and air raids, fires and demolition, and give a picture of how Tokyo must have looked before, in its wilder, less civilized days. As late as the '80s, the Yakuza tried to burn down the area so that more profitable companies could be established, but it failed, and since then bar owners and patrons have patrolled the dark, narrow alleys at night.

Most of all, Golden Gai resembles the house in the Ghibli film *Howl's Moving Castle*. It squeaks, creaks, sputters and sighs, and sometimes, when it's really late, you can swear it was moving. Here is a horror-movie bar called **Deathmatch in Hell** next to a bar with an antiquarian theme known for its lemon *kakigori*, which in turn is built under a bar for film workers that once featured in Wim Wender's documentary *Tokyo-Ga*. And in a narrow alley between them all: a bar completely dressed in leopard print that plays '80s music and also happens to make fantastic ramen. Here there are bars specializing in jazz, soul, punk and flamenco, and bars for fans of horseracing, plastic models, S&M sex and the board game Go. Wherever you look, you see a new world. And that's what makes it so fun. So don't plan too much before a visit. Let the moving castle take you where it wants.

Despite its rundown exterior, however, Golden Gai is not separated from the rest of Japan. So the same things that apply elsewhere also apply here. The area even has a few more rules: you aren't allowed to take photos, for example; or shout or climb the buildings. Some places only accept members and regulars, and some don't want tourists. It is their right, so don't get angry, just politely elbow your way to the next place instead. There are 249 more to try.

PRACTICALITIES

My first visit to Tokyo came as a shock. Although I had traveled a lot before, it felt like visiting another planet. Everything was new and incomprehensible. No one spoke English. Signs and menus were in Japanese and you had to be Alan Turing to decipher the subway maps; and on top of that, they had three (or four) completely separate subway systems! All my energy went to finding things, thinking about which side of the escalator I had to stand on and if it was ok to drink coffee while walking. So to, hopefully, make it a little easier for you, I have gathered some practical information.

- When booking flights, look for routes operated by Japanese airlines – they have better food and you get to bring two suitcases per person.
- Flights to Haneda airport are preferable to those to Narita, because Haneda is closer to town and has better restaurants.
- Most hotels in Tokyo are clean, so it is possible to get away with a cheaper hotel room even if the room is very likely to be tiny.
- The advantages of a more expensive hotel are that you usually get a fantastic view of the city, and that they have a hotel bar and concierge service – a pretty big advantage when it comes to Tokyo.
- Tokyo is a good city for Airbnb. The rooms are generally clean, safe and have high-tech key systems, so you don't have to meet up with landlords.
- Another great advantage of Airbnb is that you can live in cozy residential areas such as Nakameguro, Daikanyama and Ebisu, while most hotels are located in crazy-busy places like Shibuya and Shinjuku. Instead, you can go there when you feel like it.
- If you have plans to leave Tokyo and travel around on the *shinkansen* (Japanese high-speed bullet train), check if you will save money by getting a Japan Rail Pass. They are much cheaper for tourists, even if you have to pre-order it before leaving home.
- Also pre-order a portable internet device that you pick up at the airport when you arrive and leave in a mailbox when you go. It's simple and cheap, and constant internet connection is actually a must if you want to find a single place in this book.
- Take out cash at one of the international ATMs as soon as you land at the airport. Many places in Japan do not accept cards and it may take a while before you find another machine that works. Otherwise, the safest bets are ATMs at Japanese post offices or 7-Elevens. There are also some Family Marts and Lawsons that take international cards, but certainly not all of them.
- Buy an *onigiri* and an iced tea and breathe a little before it's time to go in to town.
- There are several options to get to and from the airport. In general, however, taxis are expensive and unnecessary, and if you are staying near one of the stops for the limousine bus, I like it more than the subway. It takes a little longer but is calmer, has wifi and views, plus you don't have to lug around your suitcase when you change lines at large metro stations.

- Sooner or later, however, you will take the metro or bus, so get yourself a Suica or Pasmo card as quickly as possible. They work on all lines and save you a lot of hassle, are easy to top up – even if you have to do it with cash – and you can use them to buy things at the convenience store.
- Also, equip yourself with patience before learning how to interpret the subway system. There are special apps for this, but I still haven't found a good one.
- The subway rush hours are 7–9am and 5–7pm, and most lines stop at midnight. There are also special carriages for women and seats for the elderly and the disabled – please, don't sit on these, it'll be embarrassing and awkward for you.
- And yes, you stand on the left on escalators in Japan.
- Don't talk loudly or eat on the subway. Also don't eat while walking – so I still don't really understand where you're supposed to gobble up all the food you buy at the convenience stores.
- Google Maps is a Tokyo traveler's best friend. Use it to find restaurants, shops and, not least, the right subway exit. The stations are so huge that going out wrong exits can be disastrous.
- Smoking is allowed inside many bars, izakayas and BBQ places, but not outdoors. In this case, find a smoking room.
- Trash cans can be difficult to find, but there are always some outside the nearest convenience store. Do not under any circumstance underestimate the convenience stores. They have everything you need and are open 24/7. There is at least one in every neighborhood and they have incredibly good food as well (p. 123–125).
- When you pay, place your card or cash in the small bowl on the counter. Accept the receipt and change with both hands. It's polite. Say thank you with a simple "*Arigato*" or "Thank you", but don't put your hands together and bow like in Thailand, it is probably appreciated but a little over the top in Japan.
- Internet bookings are quite unusual in Japan, so if you can't email you must call and book a table, which can be difficult, because many Japanese people don't speak English. In that case, it is probably easiest to ask the hotel concierge to book a table for you. My favorite method, however, is to simply walk past the restaurant and check if they have a table for later in the week.
- To get a table at the most popular places, there's now a bunch of concierge services on the internet. However, they always charge an exorbitant fee and feel like a scam, so avoid these.
- Never transfer food from chopsticks to chopsticks and never stick chopsticks into the rice between bites, instead place them on the edge of your bowl or plate or on the table like a normal person.
- And please, don't hold the chopsticks with your fingers so close to the thinner end, as though you are holding a pencil or something.
- The complicated Japanese toilets are a chapter in themselves. But in short, 小 means small flush and 大 big flush. If you press おしり it will spray water on your bum and ビデ on your hooha.
- To ask for the bill, cross your index fingers. I promise, it's not a joke.
- Speaking of hand signals, when pointing, do so with your entire hand. It's rude to point with your index finger.
- And remember that in Japan they don't tip.

INDEX

7-Eleven 123

Afuri 14
Ahiru Store 152
Akaoni 104
Akira Nakameguro 55
Another8 154

Bar Gen Yamamoto 166
Bar High Five 164
Bar Martha 168
Bear Pond 130
Ben Fiddich 166
Bondy 68
Butagumi 86

Café de l'Ambre 138
Camelback 132
Centre the Bakery 121
Chilita 165
Curry Kusamakura 66

Delifucious 114
Dominique Ansel
   Bakery 121
Dosanjin 28
Drinkers Alley 108
Drunkards Alley 108
Dylan 68

Ebisu Yokocho 107
Ethiopia 68

Fuglen 131
Fuku Yakitori 53

Gem by Moto 157
Gen Gen An 144
Ginza Noodles Clam
   Ramen 19
Ginza Shimada 104
Golden Gai 169
Gyoza no Yasubei 77

Harajuku Gyoza Ro 74
Hatos Bar 154
Hatos Outside 66
Henry's Burger 114
Himitsudo 120
Honke Ponga 43

Ichiran 117

Jiromaru 42

Kama-Asa 33
Kaneko Hannosuke 30
Kappabashi Kitchen
   Town 33
Kikanbo 15
Koffee Mameya 135
Konjiki Hototogisu 18
Korea Town 47
Kushiwakamaru 52

Land Curry & Coffee 65
Little Nap Coffee Stand 133
Little Smith 164

Matsuya 117
Memory Lane 56

Nakana Beer Kobo 154
Nakiryu 12
Nemuro Hanamaru 95
Niku Yokocho 45
Nonbei Yokocho 108

Ohka the Best Days 78
Omoide Yokocho 56
Omotesando Koffee 134
Oniyanma 28
Onoda Shoten 41

Piss Alley 56
Punk Rock Izakaya 102

Rokurinsha 17

Saitamaya 55
Sakurai Japanese Tea
    Experience 143
Sanshuya 104
Satei Hato 139
Savoy 119
Shin-Okubo 47
Shin Udon 26
Soba Yakko 28
Sukiya 117
Sumibi Yakiniku
    Nakahara 38
Sushi Nakamura 97
Sushi no Midori 95
Sushi Sho Saito 97
Switch Coffee 130

Taihou 86
Tatemichiya 102

Temmaya 69
Tokyo Ramen Street 17
Tokyo Saryo 145
Tonki 84
Tonkotsu Suzuki 89
Toranomon Koffee 134
Track Bar 168
Tsukiji 33

Umi 97
Urara 133

Wagyu Mafia the Cutlet
    Sandwich 115
Winestand Waltz 153

Yakinuku Kunimoto
    Shinkan 40
Yoshinoya 117
Yurakucho Gado-shita 109

Published in 2019 by Hardie Grant Travel, a
division of Hardie Grant Publishing
First published in 2018 by Natur & Kultur,
Sweden
Original title: Tokyo för Foodisar

Hardie Grant Travel (Melbourne)
Building 1, 658 Church Street
Richmond, Victoria 3121

Hardie Grant Travel (Sydney)
Level 7, 45 Jones Street
Ultimo, NSW 2007

www.hardiegrant.com/au/travel

**A catalogue record for this
book is available from the
National Library of Australia**

Tokyo for Food Lovers
ISBN 9781741176629

10 9 8 7 6 5 4 3 2 1

Publisher
Melissa Kayser

Project editor
Megan Cuthbert

Translator
Helena Holmgren

Editor
Alison Proietto

Editorial assistance
Aimee Barrett and Rosanna Dutson

Typesetting
Megan Ellis

Prepress
Megan Ellis and Splitting Image Colour Studio

Printed in China by 1010 Printing International
Limited